25 Lessons in Mindfulness is a gem. Stmoment, Ameli takes us on a journey mindfulness. Written with grace, comp chapter is helpful. Every chapter gives us a new a... It is a book that I will treasure and recommend to friends, family, colleagues, and patients.

—ROBERT L. LEAHY, PHD, Director, American Institute for Cognitive Therapy; Clinical Professor of Psychology, Department of Psychiatry, Weill Cornell University Medical College, New York Presbyterian Hospital; author of *The Worry Cure, Anxiety Free,* and *Beat the Blues Before They Beat You*

In this very practical book, Ameli, a superb teacher of the art, craft, and science of mindfulness, offers a step-by-step guide for those who are not lucky enough to attend her celebrated mindfulness classes in person.

—NORMAN E. ROSENTHAL, MD, Clinical Professor of Psychiatry at Georgetown; author of *Transcendence and Winter Blues*

Organized around a rich set of practices and clearly articulated teachings, this book will serve anyone seeking to cultivate a compassionate, wise, and mindful presence.

—TARA BRACH, PHD, author of *Radical Acceptance and True Refuge*

A triumph! In this groundbreaking book, Ameli has seamlessly merged East and West by bringing a rigorous, scientific mind to ancient spiritual practices. A must-read for anyone who wants to understand the logic behind the mind–body connection and who is seeking powerful tools for living a full, vibrant, purposeful life.

—ALICIA KORTEN, CEO, The Culture Company; author of *Change Philanthropy*

In this wonderfully practical guide, Ameli, a leader in promoting the positive benefits of mindfulness for depression, anxiety, and other problems of living, provides step-by-step instructions for a number of mindfulness techniques. Anyone looking for a good introduction to mindfulness and the ways it can transform one's life will find this book a great resource.

—STEPHEN J. F. HOLLAND, PSYD, Director, Capital Institute for Cognitive Therapy, Washington, DC; coauthor of *Treatment Plans and Interventions for Depression and Anxiety Disorders*

This excellent book has everything you need to get started in practicing mindfulness. I highly recommend it.

—NICHOLAS LORE, founder of the counseling field of career coaching; author of *The Pathfinder*

Ameli weaves together the rigor of science, the wisdom of reflection, and the beauty of art, offering a new way of living that has the power to transform our individual and collective lives.

—SHAUNA L. SHAPIRO, PHD, associate professor, Santa Clara University; coauthor of *The Art and Science of Mindfulness*

If you are interested in learning about mindfulness in a way that informs you of the latest research and illustrates the fundamentals through examples and anecdotes, this book will provide all you need. Ameli writes from a strong intellectual understanding but also from inspiration created by her own experiences.

—JONATHAN FOUST, founder, Meditation Teacher Training Institute; Guiding Teaching, Insight Meditation Community of Washington; senior teacher and former president, Kripalu Center for Yoga and Health

25 Lessons in Mindfulness

25 Lessons in
Mindfulness
Now Time for Healthy Living

Rezvan Ameli, PhD

American Psychological Association
Washington, DC

The views expressed in this book do not necessarily represent the views of the NIMH or
the United States government.

Published by
American Psychological Association
750 First Street, NE
Washington, DC 20002
www.apa.org

To order
APA Order Department
P.O. Box 92984
Washington, DC 20090-2984
Tel: (800) 374-2721; Direct: (202) 336-5510
Fax: (202) 336-5502; TDD/TTY: (202) 336-6123
Online: www.apa.org/pubs/books
E-mail: order@apa.org

In the U.K., Europe, Africa, and the Middle East, copies may be ordered from
American Psychological Association
3 Henrietta Street
Covent Garden, London
WC2E 8LU England

Typeset in Sabon by Circle Graphics, Inc., Columbia, MD

Printer: Edwards Brothers, Inc., Ann Arbor, MI
Cover Designer: Naylor Design, Washington, DC

The opinions and statements published are the responsibility of the authors, and such
opinions and statements do not necessarily represent the policies of the American
Psychological Association.

Library of Congress Cataloging-in-Publication Data

Ameli, Rezvan.
  25 Lessons in mindfulness: Now time for healthy living / Rezvan Ameli. — First edition.
     pages cm
  Includes bibliographical references and index.
  ISBN 978-1-4338-1323-8 — ISBN 1-4338-1323-8 1. Psychotherapy—Religious
aspects—Buddhism. 2. Meditation—Therapeutic use. 3. Meditation—Buddhism—
Psychology. I. Title.
  RC489.M43A44 2013
  616.89'14—dc23
                                        2012051511

British Library Cataloguing-in-Publication Data
A CIP record is available from the British Library.

Printed in the United States of America
First Edition

http://dx.doi.org/10.1037/14257-000

To my friend Afsaneh, for her courage and radiance.

Grace

When the white mouthed waves of outrage and anguish
bow into the distance
and give way to stillness,
When the sharp teeth of wounds and fears
loosen their grip on the flesh
and give way to tranquility,
I swim freely among the wonderful creatures of the depth
with gratitude.

—*Rezvan Ameli, 2007*

CONTENTS

ACKNOWLEDGMENTS

I acknowledge and thank loved ones, teachers, friends, colleagues, and participants in my classes and groups. I also thank those who have been a part of difficult life experiences. They have helped me face, understand, and learn to appreciate all experience. Indeed, I acknowledge everyone who has come into my life, for each has been a teacher. I would not be who I am or where I am without them. I am deeply grateful for my life as it is.

I would like to express special thanks to my friend Sophia GlezosVoit, who offered her generous help when I really needed it; Randy Schools and Kallie Wasserman of NIH-R&W, who provided the opportunity and administrative assistance to offer mindfulness classes; and Victor Landa of Shanti Yoga Center for Harmony, who provided the home and the venue for these classes.

25 Lessons in
Mindfulness

INTRODUCTION

Sarah was an articulate and eloquent woman who worked harder and did better than anyone she knew. In telling me this, she wasn't being boastful. It was just a fact. All that mattered to her in life, even when she was a child, was to be productive and perfect. This mattered more than sleep, exercise, relationships, and good-quality food. But the effects of her self-imposed stress were starting to show. The quality of her life was in a steep decline, and she felt so tense and anxious at work that even the sight of the office building made her cringe. She spent more and more time at work, and her family suffered too.

I met Sarah at a mindfulness class that I taught in 2009. She signed up in the hopes of achieving some measure of balance in her life. At the end of the 8-week session, she admitted to the group that she had had doubts at the outset of the course that any meditation class could be of much value to her. But each week, she diligently applied what she was learning, and to her amazement, for the first time in her life she could slow down, relax, and let go of the inner pressures that drove her. Her marriage improved, and her children were more relaxed when interacting with her. Even her work was better, and the overall quality of her life felt rewarding. She no longer felt nervous when she arrived to work in the morning.

This book offers practices and concepts that can help you to apply the ancient but ever-current mindfulness tools that proved so valuable to Sara and countless others. The practices and concepts that are presented in this book are those that I have found informative, helpful, and transformative in my own life and the lives of others.

Your specific story might be vastly different from Sarah's. Yet, tangible sources of stress, a desire to cope better with life, and a wish to suffer less and enjoy more are common threads that have brought people to my classes. Mindfulness has helped participants to cope with stress in many areas of their lives, including work and school; health issues such as coping with illness; interpersonal problems; parenting and marital issues; juggling tasks and responsibilities; confusion about goals and future direction; existential questions about what really matters in life; living with sick children or elderly parents; politics of the work place; prioritizing various demands on one's time, energy, and emotional resources; and not drawing joy and pleasure from life when nothing obvious is wrong or lacking.

The essence of mindfulness is to pay attention to your present-moment experiences with an accepting and friendly attitude—to notice, to allow, and to observe what is happening in each moment with curiosity and openness, whether the experience is pleasant, unpleasant, or neutral. Jon Kabat-Zinn, Professor of Medicine Emeritus and founding director of the Stress Reduction Clinic and the Center for Mindfulness in Medicine, Healthcare, and Society at the University of Massachusetts Medical School, defined *mindfulness* as paying attention on purpose, in the present, and nonjudgmentally to the unfolding of experience moment by moment (Kabat-Zinn, 2005).

When was the last time you chewed very slowly and really tasted and sensed the fragrance of a single grape, a cherry, or a bite of apple with your complete attention? How often do you take the time to notice the sensation of the cloth from your clothing on your skin? Have you been conscious of the felt sensation of wool, cotton, or silk? Have you ever brought your full attention to a single breath and closely followed it from the beginning to the end? How do the bottoms of your feet feel? Have you noticed the way in which you balance your weight on the four corners of your feet? Do you pay attention to the components of a single step—lift, move, and place as you step forward? How about the sensations from stepping backwards or sideways? Do you ever bring your full attention, curiosity, and open attitude to a pain experience, or do you rather quickly and automatically decide to reach for the bottle of ibuprofen or some other remedy? Attention to and acceptance of these everyday experiences help to increase our awareness of the present moment. The idea is not to judge or evaluate these experiences, but simply to notice them. By doing so, we experience less anxiety about the future or rumination about the past. We release fears and preoccupations because staying mindful requires refocusing our attention on the present moment—again and again. Thich Nhat Hanh (1992b), a devoted mindfulness practitioner, philosopher, monk, prolific writer, and poet, put it beautifully and simply when he said that mindfulness is to breathe in and to know you are breathing in and to breath out and know that you are breathing out.

Mindfulness is about noticing the present moment with a conscious mind and a compassionate, open, and loving heart. When mindfulness is brought to its core, two essential parts remain: (a) to notice and (b) to accept and appreciate what is noticed. The consciousness witnesses, observes, and stays put, without grasping, and allows each moment to flow in and to flow out so that the next moment can fully flow in. Along with the conscious, aware, and witnessing mind, we bring forth the intention to be kind, friendly, accepting, generous, gentle, loving, and grateful to every experience and to each sensation, thought, or feeling as it unfolds under the gaze of our attention. In this way of being, mindfulness invites us to treasure our experience in each moment as if it were our first and our last—an immeasurably precious gift worthy of full attention. We all have the capacity to know what is happening in the body, mind, and heart in each moment, and we also have the capacity to accept and befriend what we notice. Mindfulness gives us the tools to fully engage in our experiences and to live life without censorship.

To put it simply, the two major components of mindfulness are (a) focused attention and (b) a quality of openness and positivity in the heart that is usually described with words such as *compassion* and *love*. Make no mistake: Compassion, love, and focused attention are not for the faint of heart. Their integration into our daily life requires determination and discipline. It also requires guidance. This book is written with the intention of helping you to integrate mindfulness into your daily life.

To dispel any misconceptions, mindfulness does not require any particular religious or cultural belief system. You need not buy into any particular concept, philosophy, or religion. You need not be altruistic or have grand ideas about the universe. You need not be a hippie, a monk, or "new agey" to practice mindfulness. Preschoolers and successful CEOs alike have benefited from this practice. Mindfulness is simple but not easy. It is simple because we all have the capacity to be mindful. It is not easy because it requires discipline. Like our muscles, the capacity for mindfulness requires regular work to retain its strength, tone, and versatility. It is something we acquire only with practice. We all have the capacity to be mindful; it is something that we can enhance, cultivate, and reinforce. It is versatile and can be applied to all life experiences, such as breathing, walking, sounds, sights, eating, emotions, and thoughts. Sitting in meditation is only one form of mindfulness practice.

Time and again it has been shown that regular and consistent use and application of a mindful approach to daily life experiences reduces stress. Mindfulness is all about self-care. It is a very special form of self-care in that it will inevitably also benefit the people who come in contact with you directly or indirectly. Mindfulness can enhance self-care and well-being physically, psychologically, and even spiritually.

The most explicit descriptions of mindfulness were detailed in the teachings of the Buddha about 2,500 years ago. The true origins of mindfulness and meditative and reflective practices go back much further, probably to prehistoric religious practices in India and Persia. Although mindfulness is a timeless practice that, in one form or another, has been recommended throughout the history of humankind, interest in mindfulness and its related practices in the West has blossomed greatly in recent years. Scientists, clinicians, doctors, educators, individual practitioners, the military, and even politicians are attesting to the value of this simple but effective practice. Indeed, in his recent book, *A Mindful Nation,* Ohio Congressman Tim Ryan (2012) called the growing attention to mindfulness and its effectiveness "a quiet revolution" (p. xvii). He described his own firsthand experiences with mindfulness as well as the potential for integrating it into the nation's educational system, health system, and the military.

Thousands of years of experience and knowledge in the East and recent scientific advances in the West confirm the health benefits of mindfulness and related practices. Jon Kabat-Zinn, with his vision and effort, successfully brought mindfulness to the folds of Western medical practice through a combination of techniques and practices known as mindfulness-based stress reduction. The application of mindfulness in medicine has vastly increased in recent years. There are now centers at Stanford University, University of Wisconsin, Emory University, University of California–Los Angeles, University of Miami, Duke University, University of Arizona, and Harvard, to name a few, that study contemplative neuroscience, compassion, altruism, integrative medicine, and positive psychology and that are supported by both governmental and private funding sources. Mindfulness is central to almost all contemplative practices. Recent studies have addressed the impact of various forms of mindfulness, meditation, forgiveness, and loving-kindness on the function and structure of the brain and the nervous system, the immune system, the respiratory system, and the cardiovascular system. These investigations point to the importance of cultivating positive human attributes such as love, compassion, forgiveness, and altruism, as well as to the effectiveness of reflective and mindfulness practices such as meditation in promoting, enhancing, and maintaining health and well-being. The question is no longer, "Does mindfulness work?" We know it does. The questions have become much more specific. I recall preparing for a lecture on mindfulness in 2009. When I checked the government-funded investigations on the topic, I found about 60 studies. One year later, the number had increased to about 90. In May 2011, the number had risen to over 180 and in November 2012 to over 280 (http://www.clinicaltrials.gov). These studies cover a large array of scientific questions using various forms and aspects of mindfulness, such as mindful sitting, breathing, eating, listening, walking, and compassion-focused techniques. Many studies focus on medical and psychiatric conditions. Some studies are exploring the impact of mindfulness on specific cardiovascular, respiratory, immune, and nervous system disorders. Others are investigating the impact of mindfulness on addictions, drug- and alcohol-related problems, pain management, eating disorders and problems related to weight control, mood disorders and depression, various forms of anxiety disorders, suicidal behavior, and even psychosis. There are studies on the use of mindfulness in children, adolescents, adults, and older people. The use and impact of mindfulness techniques in education is another interesting area of research. The results in these various areas of investigation are quite promising.

It is important to emphasize practice. Knowledge alone isn't enough to bring about transformation. Indeed, knowledge is rarely what is lacking when you are trying to cultivate skills that require firsthand experience. The new advancements in the media connect us to unbelievably rich sources of written information, readily available with a few clicks of a button, using powerful search engines such as Google, Yahoo, Bing, and others without the need for any books. What's more, most of us know what does and does not help us, and yet we still do not follow our instincts to cultivate what our knowledge dictates. To take good care of ourselves, we need to know, but we also need to experiment and experience. Experiencing and practicing mindfulness, as I describe in this book, can be a transformative step in the direction of self-care.

This book can be of value to the novice, to the experienced practitioner, and to the teachers of mindfulness. Those of you who are novices can use this book to develop and practice your own preferred and unique combination of mindfulness techniques. You will be guided through the process of integrating mindfulness into your daily life. To succeed in practice development, you will need to suspend judgment about the techniques while learning and integrating mindfulness into day-to-day routines. Those of you who are experienced practitioners can use this book to enrich and deepen your current practice. Finally, those of you who teach mindfulness can implement and tailor the practices to individuals or groups.

Before the 25 practice lessons, I provide three brief introductory chapters. Chapter 1 summarizes the scientific findings about the effects of mindfulness on health and well-being. Chapter 2 discusses the philosophy behind mindfulness, especially Buddhist theories about the source of suffering. I invite you to look beyond this volume for a more in-depth examination of these topics. The literature is vast, and research is accumulating as we speak. This book's greatest contributions are its emphasis on experience and practice development and its detailed descriptions of techniques. The focus on practice development is born out of many years of my own personal experiences, the experiences of other teachers and practitioners of meditation, and the experiences of class participants who wanted to incorporate mindfulness into their lives regularly. Many of us have experienced a zigzag rather than a straight line in our efforts to develop a regular practice. Only a minority starts practicing and immediately gets the hang of it. Most of us have needed to mindfully attend to, sit with, and embrace the initial difficulty of developing regular practice. In that vein, Chapter 3 provides basic tips and a suggested approach for building a practice.

Consistent with the two main elements of mindfulness—focused attention and compassion—the bulk of the book is devoted to two sets of practices: attentional skills and the development of compassion. Specific teachings are provided in the form of lessons. Lessons 1 through 17 build basic attentional skills. We start with mindful breathing (Lesson 1), the most basic and important lesson, and then use alternative anchors for focusing the attention, such as other body sensations, sounds, walking, and eating (Lessons 2–12). We return to mindful breathing by considering five additional practices that call attention to the breath (Lessons 13–17). The justification for providing several lessons on the subject of breathing techniques lies in the connection between the breath and the brain, immune system, cardiovascular system, and respiratory system. The connection between breath and health has strong roots in both the yogic teachings of the East and the more recent scientific advances by the practitioners and researchers of the West. We then focus on the development of an attitude of love and compassion, the general feelings of acceptance and positivity in the heart (Lessons 18–25). Although I recommend completing one lesson at a time, the various lessons are not discrete learnings. Rather, they will all eventually blend into a more conscious and caring experience of the self and the other and a greater appreciation for the full spectrum of all life experiences.

To develop a mindfulness practice, an overarching and crucial approach is to set aside judgment (or skepticism or expectation) about the various techniques until after you have practiced them a sufficient number of times. Even if initially you believe you dislike a certain activity or feel skeptical, try to stay with the guidelines. Buying into judgment is among the greatest sources of stress and can impede your willingness and zest to explore simple and effective means of self-care and self-healing. Judgment is natural and will arise, but we need to stay aware of it so that it does not color our mind with doubt and disbelief or take control of what we will or will not do. The mindful approach is neither to push judgment away nor to treat our judgment as facts; rather, the mindful approach is to observe and acknowledge our experience of judgment and then continue what we set out to do. To benefit from the practices, you need to approach this book with an open heart, an open mind, and a willingness to engage in the practices as outlined.

Relaxing judgment and expectations? How can one expect nothing from the practices that promise so much? This is the inherent paradox in the practice of mindfulness. The attitudes of judgment and expectation can work against mindfulness development. Judgments and expectations are exactly the kind of thinking patterns that we want to stay conscious of and ultimately modify through mindfulness practice because they increase dissatisfaction and negative emotions, which in turn create or increase stress.

A regular practice of mindfulness—the practice of standing side by side with and being aware of our experiences—provides the possibility of fully engaging in our whole life, not only a fraction of it. Mindfulness helps us embrace pleasant, unpleasant, or neutral experiences evenhandedly. We are reminded time and again that the breath, sights, sounds, sensations, emotions, and thoughts—all experiences that get interpreted as pleasant, unpleasant, or neutral experiences—are the universal and inevitable ingredients of our humanity, our so-called human condition. We learn to observe, befriend, and engage in our human condition with openness and appreciation. We will try to open our arms to even those experiences that we do not typically perceive as pleasant on the surface, such as pain, fear, anger, or restlessness. By bringing attention and compassion to such experiences, we will learn to relate to them in a new way. What we experience in response to a specific trigger in a given moment is rather unique, and yet the feelings, sensations, and thoughts that are generated about the experience are universal and imbedded in our human condition. We learn that we can choose to bring our friendly and loving attention to fear, anger, despair, boredom, and joy and to the various sensations and thoughts that these states bring about. The task of mindfulness is to experience and tolerate our full humanity. We learn that we can choose to apply this form of loving attention, mindfulness, to all experience and that gradually we can even extend it to others. We learn that we can extend our mindful attention to loved ones, friends, and neighbors and with sufficient practice, to people whom we do not like or do not know personally. The more we appreciate, accept, and are open to the full experience of our humanity, the more we appreciate the similarities that we share with every human the world over or even with other species. If this sounds simple yet grand at the same time—it is. The implications are immense and mind blowing. And the most astonishing thing is that we can choose to partake in it. Every one of us can partake in this quiet revolution—a revolution that begins inside and whose benefits will naturally radiate to the outside, to loved ones, colleagues, neighbors, and communities.

Finally, a note of caution is in order. Mindfulness can be a powerful tool to enhance health and well-being. As effective as mindfulness practices can be, if you are suffering from physical ailments or psychiatric disorders, these techniques are best applied and implemented under the care and supervision of a professional. If you are experiencing any psychotic symptoms, such as delusions or hallucinations, please consult your health care provider before using any meditative practices, including mindfulness. An introduction to mindfulness practices under the care of a professional is available. Several forms of psychological treatments, such as dialectical behavior therapy (Linehan, 1993), acceptance and commitment therapy (Hayes, 2002; Hayes, Luoma, Bond, Masuda, & Lillis, 2006; Hayes, Strosahl, & Wison, 1999), mindfulness-based cognitive therapy (Segal, William, & Teasdale, 2001), and mindfulness-based stress reduction (Kabat-Zinn, 2005), make extensive use of mindfulness by trained professionals. This book is not a substitute for individualized and professional treatments.

I

WHY BE MINDFUL, AND HOW?

CHAPTER ONE

MINDFULNESS AND SCIENCE

During the last 3 decades, mindfulness has become increasingly popular both as a topic for research and as an adjunctive treatment for physical, psychiatric, and stress-related disorders. Several meta-analyses that summarized some of the research are frequently cited in the literature. A *meta-analysis* is a statistical technique that combines research findings from a number of studies and assists in conducting a systematic review of a subject matter. For example, a meta-analysis may examine several clinical trials of a certain treatment in an effort to obtain a better understanding of how well the treatment works.

One meta-analysis of mindfulness was done by Ruth Baer (2003), a researcher from the University of Kentucky. She combined the results of 22 studies and concluded that mindfulness-based techniques may be helpful in the treatment of several disorders, such as anxiety, depression, binge eating, chronic pain, fibromyalgia, and psoriasis. In another meta-analysis, Grossman, Niemann, Schmidt, and Walach (2004) combined 20 studies that met their 11-point inclusion criteria with a total of 1,605 subjects. They selected studies that were written in the English language, used quantitative measures of outcome, and had control groups. In these studies, mindfulness was taught in groups, class sessions were between 6 and 12 weeks in length, and classes lasted at least 2.5 hours. The results supported the positive effects of mindfulness on such disorders as chronic pain, fibromyalgia, cancer, and coronary artery disease.

Another meta-analysis, by Hofmann, Sawyer, Witt, and Oh (2010), focused on the impact of mindfulness on depression and anxiety. They identified 727 studies, of which 39 met their selection criteria with a total of 1,140 patients. They selected studies that included adult participants who had a variety of psychological or medical diagnoses, used a qualitative measure of depression or anxiety, and used either mindfulness-based cognitive therapy (MBCT) or mindfulness-based stress reduction (MBSR). They concluded that the pre- and posttreatment comparisons demonstrated that mindfulness was an effective treatment for reducing symptoms of anxiety and depression.

The impact of meditative, contemplative, and mindfulness practice on the brain and the nervous system has been the subject of a whole host of studies (Davidson, 2010; Davidson et al., 2003; Hölzel et al., 2008, 2010, 2011; Lazar et al., 2005; Lutz, Brefczynski-Lewis, Johnstone, & Davidson, 2008; Lutz, Dunne, & Davidson, 2007; Lutz, Greischar, Perlman, & Davidson, 2009; Lutz, Greischar,

Rawlings, Ricard, & Davidson, 2004; Nauert, 2010; Newberg et al., 2010; Siegel, 2007). The renowned neuroscientist Richard Davidson of University of Wisconsin–Madison and colleagues have studied the effects of meditation and contemplative work, including compassion, on the brain for many years. These researchers have established that there are both functional and structural brain changes that could be attributed to the impact of meditation.

In one study, Lutz et al. (2004) compared the brain activity of long-time Buddhist meditators with a group of control subjects. The long-time meditators had anywhere from 10,000 to 50,000 hours of meditation practice, whereas the control subjects had 1 week of meditation practice. They put electrodes on the scalp of all subjects to measure brain activity during meditation. They demonstrated that long-time Buddhist meditators produced more significant changes in their brain wave patterns than did the control subjects. In particular, long-time meditators produced high-amplitude gamma activity during meditation. These effects were particularly strong for lateral frontoparietal electrode sites. The authors concluded that their data suggested that meditation involved temporal integrative mechanisms that induced short- and long-term neural changes.

Lazar from Harvard University and collaborators (Lazar et al., 2005) have reported that meditation is associated with increased cortical thickness in a subset of cortical regions related to sensory, cognitive, and emotional processing. In addition, regular practice of meditation was associated with slowing down of age-related thinning of the frontal cortex. They studied experienced meditators who on average had 9 years of experience and practiced on average 6 hours per week. They compared these meditators with nonmeditators.

They measured the cortical thickness in the two groups with well-established cortical measurement approaches. The cortical thickness change was not uniform across all brain regions; instead, it was specific to the Brodmann areas 9 and 10. Brodmann areas were originally defined and numbered by the German anatomist Korbinian Brodmann in 1909.

Even a relatively short period of practice, a 2-month course in MBSR that combines several practices, including yoga, meditation, and compassion practice, produced measurable changes in the brain and the immune function in positive ways. In a study by Davidson et al. (2003), subjects were randomly assigned to either an MBSR or a wait-list group. After the MBSR course, both groups received the flu vaccine. The researchers found that individuals who participated in MBSR courses demonstrated a significantly greater left-sided anterior activation of the brain that is associated with positive affect. They further found that the MBSR group had a greater antibody response to the influenza vaccine.

Since these initial studies, a number of other research findings have confirmed the impact of mindfulness meditation on the brain (Hölzel et al., 2011). Interestingly, even a brief period of training (30 minutes) designed to cultivate positive qualities such as equanimity and loving-kindness has produced alterations in emotion regulation and brain functions (Urry et al., 2003). The effect of meditative practices on the brain continues to be studied by well-known researchers. The brain function and structural changes influence the autonomic nervous system, the endocrine system, and the immune system, which suggests that meditation can affect physical and psychological functioning.

Many authors believe that mindfulness exerts its healing effect through emotion regulation. Indeed, a substantial body of research focuses on the impact of meditative practices on emotion regulation. A special issue of the American Psychological Association's journal *Emotion* was devoted to the topic of mindfulness and emotion regulation ("Mindfulness training and emotional regulation," 2010). Various authors contributed to this issue and provided reports of the impact of mindfulness on response to sadness, social anxiety, pain, suicidal ideation, working memory, depression, positive, and negative emotions. D. M. Davis and Hayes (2011) from Pennsylvania State University summarized some of the more recent findings. In this review, they reported that mindfulness and meditative practices are found to reduce rumination and negative emotions, elicit positive emotions, reduce stress, boost working memory, enhance attentional skills, decrease emotional reactivity, increase cognitive flexibility, and increase relationship satisfaction. Lutz et al. (2007) identified qualities such as kindness, compassion, and equanimity as the qualities that are cultivated and enhanced by mental training and attentional processes.

There has been an explosion of studies in the field of psychoneuroimmunology suggesting that the biological mechanism through which meditation enhances health and well-being is the body's cellular and molecular defense mechanisms known as the *immune system,* which is regulated in part by the nervous system. Similarly, the adverse impact of stress on health and well-being has been well established. The literature is vast and overwhelming and leaves no doubt that negative emotions and stress have an adverse impact and that positive emotions contribute to health and longevity (Chida &

Steptoe, 2009, 2010; Cohen, Janicki-Deverts, & Miller, 2007; Danner, Snowdon, & Friesen, 2001; Fredrickson, 2001; Fredrickson, Cohn, & Finkel, 2008; Friedberg, Suchday, & Srinivas, 2009; Jacobs et al., 2011; Kabat-Zinn, 2003; Kabat-Zinn et al., 1998; Kiecolt-Glaser, 2009; Kubzansky, Davidson, & Rozanski, 2005; Lawler et al., 2005; Lawler-Row, Karremans, Scott, Edlis-Matityahou, & Edwards, 2008; Sapolsky, 1998; Segerstrom & Miller, 2004; Steptoe, Dockray, & Wardle, 2009; Toussaint, Owen, & Cheadle, 2012; Tugade, Fredrickson, & Feldman Barrett, 2004; Vaillant, 2008; Xu & Roberts, 2010).

The stress-response system evolved to help us respond to dangerous and life-threatening situations. For the modern human, however, much of what triggers the stress response is no longer life-or-death situations. Much lesser evils, such as negative emotional reactions to ongoing minor life events, including irritation, frustration, humiliation, and fear of social rejection, can elicit the stress response in the body. Such ongoing states of chronic stress affect the brain and its functioning and can bring about physical and psychological exhaustion, loss of motivation, loss of vitality and zest for life, an inability to relax, feelings of being on edge or keyed up even when ready to relax, and physical ailments related to the bodily systems involved in the stress reaction. Some physical stress symptoms include headache, muscle tension or pain, chest pain, fatigue, decrease in sex drive, stomach or gastrointestinal (GI) issues, and sleep problems. Stress impacts mood as well. Common symptoms of stress include anxiety, restlessness, irritability, anger, sadness, and apathy. Behavioral manifestations of stress can include interpersonal conflict, decrease or increase in eating, increase or development of nervous habits such as nail biting, drug or alcohol use, or social withdrawal. Stress has been found to be related to the development of or intensification of a number of ailments, such as pain, heart disease, GI and digestive diseases, sleep disorders, depression, anxiety disorders, obesity, autoimmune disorders, and skin problems, to name a few (Cohen et al., 2007; Sapolsky, 1998).

Stressful life experiences deregulate the immune system and interfere with and compromise the body's natural healing processes (Kiecolt-Glaser, 2009). We now know that distress can slow wound healing, diminish the strength of immune responses to vaccines, increase vulnerability to infections, reactivate latent viruses, and impact the aging process. Recent studies have shown intriguing connections among stress, feelings of helplessness, immune system impairment, and diseases such as cancer (Davidson et al., 2003; Kiecolt-Glaser, 2009; Segerstrom & Miller, 2004). A major question for research is to what extent the mind influences the increase or the decrease of specific disease processes.

Our bodies' reaction to stress is a complex and intricate response system, a survival mechanism that has evolved over millions of years. When faced with stress, hormones that increase metabolism, such as those secreted by the hypothalamus, pituitary, and adrenals, are activated and released. These hormones increase heart rate, blood pressure, and breath rate, preparing the body for fight or flight. The body's response to stress involves various systems and organs, such as the cardiovascular, musculoskeletal, nervous, and immune systems.

In addition to the stress response system, our bodies are equipped with another equally intricate and magnificent system, the ability to rest, heal, and replenish itself through what Herbert Benson, a professor, doctor, researcher, and writer, termed the *relaxation response* (Benson, 2000; Benson, Beary, & Carol, 1974). Early on, Benson studied the effects of transcendental meditation in bringing about and facilitating the body's resting and healing functions. Transcendental meditation is a form of meditation that uses a *mantra,* a sound or a short phrase, as the focus for meditation (Rosenthal, 2011). The meditator repeats the mantra internally and keeps his or her focus on it for 20 minutes twice a day. After decades of experimentation and observation, Benson (2000; Benson et al., 1974) concluded that the relaxation response can be elicited in a number of ways and has two important components: a mental device and a passive attitude. The mental device is a sound, word, object, or prayer that one chooses to focus on. The passive attitude involves not worrying about one's performance and execution of the technique, not engaging in distressing thoughts, and repeatedly returning to the mental device.

Mindfulness can certainly be considered a relaxation response. Unlike the stress response, which is instinctive and occurs via the mediation of old and archaic brain structures (subcortical parts of the brain), mindfulness requires the involvement of consciousness, a decision to focus one's attention. This conscious decision-making process takes the body out of the cycle of autonomic reactivity.

Positive psychology research has provided an important contribution to the understanding of how emotions, particularly positive emotions, affect health and longevity (Fredrickson, 2001, 2004). The eight positive emotions of love, awe, hope, compassion, faith or trust, forgiveness, joy, and gratitude are considered important factors in relief and protection from stress by regulating the neuroendocrine system (Vaillant, 2008). Cultivating positive emotions such as compassion and forgiveness is not only an altruistic or moral undertaking. Rather, these practices also enhance health and well-being by reducing stress and improving the functions of several body systems, including the cardiovascular, endocrine, and immune systems (Toussaint et al., 2012). Being forgiving and compassionate is no longer only a valued moral attribute. Research on positive emotional states and their effects on health and longevity has demonstrated that positive emotions improve health and longevity (Tugade et al., 2004).

Compassion and its implications for human health and well-being is now established as a legitimate and important field of scientific inquiry. The Center for Compassion and Altruism Research and Education at Stanford University opened in 2009 and has assembled a multidisciplinary team of researchers that includes neuroscientists, psychologists, educators, and philosophical and contemplative thinkers around the study of compassion. His Holiness the Dalai Lama has contributed financially and participated in a scientific symposium focused on Compassion in 2010. Other prominent American educational institutions, including Harvard University, the University of California at Berkeley, Columbia University, the University of Wisconsin, the University of North Carolina at Chapel Hill, and the University of Michigan, have now conducted research studies on compassion.

For example, in one government-funded study of loving-kindness, researchers from the University of North Carolina at Chapel Hill and the University of Michigan found that regular and consistent practice of loving-kindness produced daily experiences of positive emotions and feelings (Fredrickson et al., 2008). More specifically, loving-kindness meditation increased mindfulness, a sense of purpose in life, social support, and life satisfaction and decreased symptoms of illness and depression. Compassion training is associated with increased positive emotions and feelings; decreased negative emotions and feelings; decreased stress measures, including subjective distress; improved immune response; enhanced brain activation in areas involved with emotional processing and empathy; positive impact on interpersonal processes; improved symptoms of depression; reduction in social anxiety, marital conflict, and anger; improved coping with the strains of long-term caregiving; social connectedness; and decreased social isolation (Fredrickson et al., 2008).

Similar to compassion and loving-kindness, research on forgiveness has grown rapidly in recent years. Studies at the University of Miami and the Campaign for Forgiveness Research have investigated the relationship between forgiveness and psychological well-being. Researchers have found that an increase in forgiveness, as evidenced by a decrease in avoidance and revenge and an increase in benevolence, was correlated with psychological well-being, as evidenced by increased satisfaction with life, more positive mood, less negative mood, and fewer physical symptoms (Bono, McCullough, & Root, 2008). The positive impact of forgiveness on three important systems (cardiovascular, endocrine, and immune) has been reported by several researchers (Friedberg et al., 2007; Lawler et al., 2005; Lawler-Row et al., 2008; Owen, Hayward, & Toussaint, 2011; Seybold, Hill, Neumann, & Chi, 2001). Some of the information on forgiveness and its application to the promotion of health and well-being might have oversimplified the complexity of the psychological intricacies of the process of forgiveness.

Robert Enright (1996, 2001), professor of psychology at the University of Wisconsin–Madison, is an expert in using forgiveness as a form of therapy and education. In his book *Forgiveness is a Choice*, Enright (2001) provided a detailed account of the work done by him and his research group over a 15-year period. He has demonstrated that forgiveness can reduce anxiety and depression and increase self-esteem and hopefulness. According to Enright, forgiveness, when approached sensitively, systematically, and properly, benefits the forgiver more than the forgiven. Forgiveness will decrease negative emotions and bring about clarity and peace. Similarly, Robert Emmons, a psychology professor at the University of California at Davis and the editor-in-chief of the *Journal of Positive Psychology*, has studied the impact of gratitude extensively. He defined *gratitude* as wanting what we already have and suggested that people who practice gratitude regularly by keeping a journal and keeping themselves aware of all that they should be grateful for, large and small, increase their happiness set point by 25%. Sleep and energy, among other things, improve within 3 weeks of gratitude practice (Emmons, 2007).

Barbara Fredrickson, Distinguished Professor of Psychology at the University of North Carolina at Chapel Hill, has done research on the impact of positive emotions, including compassion-related practices on health and well-being. She is best known for her broaden-and-build theory of positive emotions, which has substantial empirical support (Fredrickson, 2004). This theory posits that positive emotions such as happiness, joy, compassion, and love broaden the scope of attention, improve cognition, and encourage novel, varied, and exploratory thoughts and actions. Over time, this broadened scope of awareness results in a behavioral repertoire that helps build skills and resources. This is in contrast to negative emotions, which prompt narrow, immediate survival-oriented behavior. For example, anxiety leads to the specific fight-or-flight response for immediate survival. Although positive emotions do not have any immediate survival value, the skills and resources built by broadened behavior enhance survival. In other words, negative emotions experienced during life-threatening situations narrow an individual's thought–action repertoire, whereas positive emotions present new possibilities and enhance resilience.

In summary, there is a substantial body of research that supports the benefit of mindfulness on both physical and psychological health and well-being. Research in neuroscience, psychoneuro-immunology, and clinical and positive psychology has provided strong support for the benefits of both attention- and compassion-related practices, which are considered to be the two indispensable and interrelated aspects of mindfulness.

CHAPTER TWO

BUDDHA, MINDFULNESS, STRESS, AND RELAXATION

One way to understand mindfulness is to put it in the context of the Buddha's central teachings, the Four Noble Truths (Goldstein, 2003, 2007; Gunaratana, 2012). Briefly, the first teaching or noble truth is that there is dukkha in the universe. *Dukkha* has been translated to mean suffering, stress, and dissatisfaction, a sense that things will never measure up to our expectations or to our standards and that everything changes and nothing is permanent. Even in happiness, because of its impermanent nature, dukkha is experienced. If a person is without insight into the impermanent nature of things, dukkha will persist. The second noble truth is about the origin of dukkha. Buddha taught that the origin of dukkha is attachment and delusion. Attachment—craving for what we find pleasant and avoidance of what we find unpleasant, which are the two sides of the same coin—keeps us trapped and subject to dukkha. The third noble truth is that dukkha can be ceased and stopped. And the fourth noble truth is that the road to liberation from dukkha is the Eightfold Path, which includes right view, right intention, right speech, right action, right livelihood, right effort, right mindfulness, and right concentration. Mindfulness, an attentive awareness of the reality of things (especially of the present moment), is an antidote to dukkha (i.e., to delusion and suffering).

The Buddha's teaching on mindfulness advocates that one should establish mindfulness in one's day-to-day life, maintaining a calm awareness of bodily functions, sensations and feelings, objects of consciousness (i.e., thoughts and perceptions), and consciousness itself. The practice of mindfulness supports the development of wisdom.

SOURCES OF STRESS

Pain Versus Suffering

The Buddha distinguished suffering from pain. Suffering or stress, according to the Buddha, can be something large and important, such as a major life event, or the smallest of hardships that can bring about any level of negative sensations, thoughts, or emotions, such as a brief sensation of tightness in the chest. He further described the inevitability of old age, sickness, and death, the inevitability of impermanence, which he called the *first arrow*. This is the unchangeable truth of being human, the so-called human condition, the given. These inevitable conditions bring about suffering, which at its root is experienced as bodily sensations. These uncomfortable bodily sensations could generically be considered pain of some form. What changes the pain, an inevitable bodily sensation, into suffering (dukkha, stress) is the interpretation that our minds give to the pain, which he called the *second arrow*. We are the ones who throw the second arrow. Pain is inevitable as long as we live in our human bodies, but suffering is human-made and can be stopped. It is our resistance to the inevitable, our resistance to the pain, that creates suffering. Pain is a sensation; pain plus resistance is suffering. Our resistance to accepting pain as the natural condition of being human creates the suffering. The negative thoughts, emotions, and lack of acceptance that we bring into the picture in reaction to the inevitable, the pain, promote stress and dissatisfaction. Even what we interpret as fear, anger, or sadness, when examined closely, may be revealed as a subtle or not so subtle bodily sensation or discomfort—the beating heart, the tightness in the chest, the butterflies in the stomach, the boiling blood. These sensations are less likely to cause suffering or stress when focused on mindfully in the here and now for what they are, bodily sensations, rather than the interpretations we give them.

In his influential writing, *Sathipathana Sutta,* the Buddha detailed and delineated the road to liberation from suffering through mindfulness. The Buddha's four foundations of mindfulness are mindfulness of the body, mindfulness of the thoughts, mindfulness of the emotions, and mindfulness of hindrances. These four foundations have been a rich source and the basis for much of our modern approaches to mindfulness.

Attachment

To better understand how our thoughts and emotions contribute to our suffering from the Buddha's perspective, we need to further entertain the concept of attachment. Attachment has two sides: aversion/avoidance and attraction/craving. *Aversion/avoidance* is when we want less of, and turn away from, those experiences that we find unpleasant. *Attraction/craving* is when we want more of, and turn toward, those experiences that we find pleasant. This attachment mechanism keeps us a slave to immediate bodily sensations and diminishes our ability to attend to all experience. It ultimately results in delusion (not seeing the whole panoply of our experience, or tunnel vision), hatred (being controlled by negative emotions or aversion from sources of perceived suffering), and greed (being controlled by positive emotions and an insatiable desire to have more and more of what we like at all cost to ourselves and others). Delusion, hatred, and greed cause unhappiness.

The tendency to gravitate toward the pleasant and turn away from the unpleasant is instinctive and hardwired. Indeed, it has had survival value during the course of evolution. However, the ever-expanding sources of attachment (both cravings and aversions) in modern human life have themselves become great sources of physical, psychological, and spiritual illness. To the extent that this evolutionary mechanism controls our behavior and mind states, we are vulnerable to the suffering that results from craving the pleasant and averting the unpleasant. This is different from noticing what is pleasant or unpleasant in the moment. It is attachment to the outcome that keeps us trapped in suffering. Living in the moment and living for the moment are fundamentally different experiences. The former alleviates suffering, and the latter promotes it. If we let go of our attachments (both aversions and cravings), then we can be liberated from this trap. Again, this does not prevent us from optimizing pleasant experiences in life or reducing the possibility of unpleasant experiences. To notice one's experience with open-hearted, nonjudgmental awareness—no matter the nature of that experience—is to be mindful. To be controlled by the experience by either avoidance or craving promotes suffering.

Past and Future Orientation

Another quality of the mind that causes great stress and suffering is its tendency to wander to the past or to the future. The past has passed and cannot be changed. The future is not here yet. A past orientation can bring about sadness or regret, and a future orientation can bring about anxiety. When we are fully attending to the present moment, that is, when we are mindful, there is no regret or worry; suffering and a sense of stress are thus reduced. Each moment is what it is. To live life fully, we stay present to each moment.

Often when we engage in past or future thoughts, we feel sadness, regret, fear, insecurity, anxiety, or other negative feelings that cause suffering and stress. If we notice the tendency of the mind to go to the past or to the future and instead focus on the present moment experience without additional meaning and interpretation, we can reduce our stress and suffering.

The antidote to suffering is to let go, allowing things to be as they are, and to pay attention to what is, bringing the mind to the here and now. Anything else is an illusion and a product of the mind. Regardless of content, thoughts of the past are an illusion, as are thoughts of the future. Both are in the mind and are not real. They are a fiction of the mind, made up by our mind and not a representation of reality. The only reality is what is happening right now.

Expectations

Let's look at stress from yet another angle: as the natural product of expectation. When our expectations are not met, we immediately experience feelings of frustration, irritation, anger, hatred, envy, apprehension, or fear. Ken Keyes, the late author and lecturer on personal growth and social consciousness issues, considered expectations the number one cause of human unhappiness. Here's how it works: The more we expect, the more we expose ourselves to the generation of negative feelings. The more negative feelings we generate, the more stressed we become (Keyes, 1975, 1987, 1995).

What we first need to acknowledge is that the source of these feelings is inside of us, not outside of us. Not everyone feels the same emotions in response to the same situation or event. As humans, we will inevitably feel the various human emotions such as fear, anger, and love in their various shades. At the same time, our emotions are stirred up with various intensities on the bases of our constitution and personal histories. Thus, our emotional experiences are both universal (everyone feels them at some point) and unique (not to the exact degree or in response to the same situation or event).

One important factor that differentiates our personal reactions from one another is the different set of expectations we bring to the picture on the basis of our personal histories. It is not the boss who makes you feel humiliated or unhappy. This same boss does not create the same set of emotions in all of his or her employees to the same degree, even under the same set of circumstances. It is not just the bad boyfriend or girlfriend who makes you feel angry, unwanted, or abandoned. It is not just the other person or the outside world that creates these states. The feelings come from within. And, this is good news! We are not totally at the mercy of what is put on our plates. We have a choice. There is the outside event. Then there is the inside event. The two are separate. The more we practice mindfulness, the better we come in touch with and experience their separation. By doing so, we can gain an understanding of the inside event and what we can do about it. It is natural to feel emotions in response to outside events that are continuously filtered into our being by our senses. These feelings—positive, negative or neutral—need to be held mindfully with an attitude of acceptance and compassion. Whatever the nature of the feelings and emotional experiences, you can bring awareness to them. Certainly, it is easier to bring awareness to feelings and emotions that are mild without reactivity. It is more difficult to bring the mindful attention to intense emotions. With practice, one can remain mindful even in the midst of strong emotions. This is what the Buddha was describing when he talked about liberation from suffering.

Our social conditioning teaches us to want more money, more prestige, more education, more sex, more experience, etc. Yet that conditioning only increases our worries of all that we can lose. Greed and competition are not pleasant experiences. We accumulate stuff to no end. Then we have to cope and deal with the clutter that our insatiable appetites create. Have you noticed the size of the closets in older houses versus newer ones? No closet is big enough anymore. We keep adding to our possessions, to our attachments, and to our expectations. No partner can meet our cascading needs and expectations, so we may suffer in discontent and dissatisfaction or even end our partnership and look for happiness in a new partner. No job is good enough and responds to all our needs, so we change jobs. We keep searching for novelty and new experiences; what we already have is not satisfying.

To get out of the cycle of endless expectations, unfulfilled demands, and the resulting negative emotions, we need to work on our own habitual expectations that drive us—habitual *wants* that we think of as *needs,* attachments that leave us unfulfilled and exhausted. How often do you say *I need* this or that? Is it really a need or it is a want? We must work to harmonize the inside and the outside. We must practice to become aware of our true needs and not be automatically driven by our conditioning and the wants.

In the mindfulness class that I teach, one participant dramatically transformed her relationship with her sister by modifying her expectations and letting go of her attachment to a particular outcome. She told me that giving without expecting results was a difficult concept for her. She decided to practice it in relationship with her sister. Although her sister lived only a short distance away, they were estranged from one another. She first began by calling her sister and then asked her to meet for dinner. Her sister agreed a few times and then canceled at the last minute. By minimizing expectations, she did not experience much negative emotion at the cancellations. She kept her expectations at a minimum and did not allow the mild feelings of rejection or frustration to prevent her from continued contact with her sister. She said she was even prepared for her sister to say no without feeling deterred. After about five or six tries, she decided to catch her sister on the fly without planning ahead. It worked! During dinner they talked only about the sister, her children, and her grandchildren. She was aware of her sister's habitual tendency to take charge, but she allowed her sister to make choices about where to eat, what to eat, how much to order, and even how much tip to leave. By all accounts, the dinner was a success. Over the past year, she has kept asking at the last minute and the sister has kept accepting. Gradually, the restaurants and the food selection have become a joint decision and the conversations more varied and inclusive. For the very first time in as long as she can remember, her sister called and offered to take her out to celebrate her birthday. Both sisters are now happy and pleased with the renewed connection.

The Space Between Stimulus and Response

Victor Frankl (1959), a holocaust survivor and neurologist, stated that between stimulus and response, there is a space. In that space is our power to choose our response. In our response lie our growth and our freedom. Mindfulness can provide us with the tools that we need to free ourselves from our conditioning. Even though it seems as if our thoughts and emotional reactions to events arise automatically, we can intervene. One way we can intervene is to change the way in which we view the world, that is, to change the fixed way in which we expect the world to behave. When we modify our expectations of the world, we can also relieve our minds from judgments and their associated negative emotions. If we view our wants as preferences rather than conditions that must be met—otherwise "I will be miserable"—we can loosen their grip on our mind and body and feel comfortable and whole even when the world misbehaves. When we give up the illusion that we can control people and events by means of our expectations and judgments, we become more aware of our true needs and preferences. We can then see more clearly what is real and therefore increase the chances of getting our needs met without generating a host of negative emotions that only increase our stress levels. The practice of mindfulness focuses the mind and keeps us in the present moment, free of judgment and expectations, allowing the here-and-now experience to unfold. It reduces the negative emotions that result from disappointments and frustrated expectations. This in turn will improve our relationships with our world and ourselves and greatly diminish stress in our daily lives.

With practice, conscious awareness can help us choose what happens inside of our bodies. When we notice external events that usually bring about the stress response, or even afterward when we first notice the signs of stress in the body, we can intervene and change the course of what is happening. Instead of the habitual reactivity that wreaks havoc on so many sensitive bodily systems, we can stop and become mindful. We can bring the attention from the outside to the inside and focus it on what is happening now. When we are mindful, we notice our bodily sensations, and we notice the attitude we are holding. Under the gaze of our mindful attention, we soon find that such states are impermanent. We let go and consciously, not out of automaticity or reactivity, choose what we do next. We thus free ourselves from the autonomic reactivity and enjoy the privilege of choosing a response.

In stressful situations we tend to get tangled in two ways, either by aversion and avoidance of what we perceive as negative or by craving or greed for what we perceive as positive. Mindfulness helps break these conditioned patterns and assists in developing the capacity to peacefully coexist with both the positive and the negative sensations, thoughts, and emotions. This will help separate what is experienced from our response to the experience. Our felt experience, positive or negative, will not control what we do next. We can choose our action. We can respond instead of reacting. We bring our attention from the outside to the inside. We observe and notice our thoughts, emotions, and sensations without entanglement. We stay side by side with them without pushing away, turning away, or suppressing them. We let them be. We acknowledge the presence of thoughts, emotions, and sensations and develop the ability to witness them without reactivity.

With regular practice, conditioned patterns and habits gradually break down. As our capacity for mindful life increases, we shed the automaticity with which we have lived for a long time. Mindfulness helps us choose our response rather than react out of our past conditioning.

Meditative practices have proven effective time and again to facilitate healing. One has to make a distinction between healing and cure. The power of meditation and mindfulness approaches is in the attitudinal transformation that brings about a sense of healing, whereas the expectation of cure is inherently inconsistent with such an approach. There is a paradox inherent in the benefits of meditative practices. The paradox is this: Any strong investment in the outcome of meditative practices undermines the practice itself. Cultivating nonstriving is at the heart of meditative practices. Their healing power comes from a systematic discipline and commitment to a way of being, not from engaging in one or two practices or techniques when we feel bad or want something.

CHAPTER THREE

BUILDING A MINDFULNESS PRACTICE USING THIS BOOK

To enhance the chances of success in developing and cultivating mindfulness, I recommend a significant shift in your reading habits. If you are like most people, you may read a book at bedtime and relatively quickly (e.g., reading multiple chapters in one sitting). This way of reading may be fine with most books, but not with *25 Lessons in Mindfulness*. Now that you have read the introductory chapters, the lessons will require your active participation. I invite you to read the lessons step-by-step, when you are fully awake and alert with pauses for practice and rereading.

MAKE TIME

To maximize the benefits of mindfulness, you will need to make time for regular practice. To maximize the benefits of guidance from

25 Lessons in Mindfulness, I highly recommend that you make time on a weekly and on a daily basis.

Weekly

Set aside a regular time each week. Imagine you are taking a weekly class. In this class, you will be the student and the teacher. *25 Lessons in Mindfulness* will be the lesson plan, your guide. Do not read Lesson 1 until you have come up with a regular time for your weekly class. During your weekly classes, you will work on one lesson at a time. The lessons provide you with information, practices, and exercises. Practice each lesson for at least 1 week before moving to the next lesson. To start, set aside about 1 to 2 hours for this weekly class and then adjust your availability on the basis of your progress and need. You can even invite a friend or two or a loved one to join you in this experimentation, exploration, and adventure. The presence of a supportive community, in any size, can enhance the learning and practice of mindfulness.

Daily

In addition to the weekly classes, set aside a regular time each day during which you will practice what you have learned in the weekly classes. I will expand on this latter point next and provide examples and guidelines.

MAKE A PLACE

Where will you conduct your weekly classes and daily practices? Find a place where you can have privacy and can practice without disruption, self-consciousness, or embarrassment. If possible, personalize your space of practice. In particular, items of special emotional or spiritual value can provide a subtle inner focus. Personalizing this space can add to the ambience and to your inner connection to the place where you will be practicing. The idea is to make it a place in which you will look forward to spending time. Flowers, flower essences, your favorite fabrics, wall decorations, statuettes, even a special golf ball or baseball can add to the experiential dimension of your practice space. Engaging your senses can assist you in staying present during your practice.

Those who travel frequently may want to have a selection of items handy to bring along. Including a small rug in your items of choice can help you set up your own special space even when you are away from home. Please note that most hotels forbid burning candles or incense.

COMMIT TO PRACTICE

Making time and making a place can be your first steps toward commitment to a mindful practice. You may find that you need to be very creative to make the time and or the place. You may find that you need to make seasonal adjustments. One participant in the mindfulness class that I teach used the small deck of his apartment during the late spring and summer months. He and his wife lived in small quarters, and they had to make several conscious choices to accommodate his practice needs during the cold months of the year. They moved and shifted furniture pieces several times to come up with a 2 × 2-foot space that they both agreed on. Consider your practice a worthwhile experiment. Suspend judgment until you have practiced for a few weeks. As the benefits of practice become gradually more obvious, you will find that it is easier to make choices that facilitate your practice. One helpful strategy is to commit to a period of time and recommit at the end of your chosen time frame. For example, commit to practice for 1 week at a time and renew your commitment on a weekly basis. This will also allow you to incorporate any shifts and changes regarding your practice.

In most mindfulness trainings and workshops in the United States and elsewhere, the initial training spans several weeks. Each session lasts 2.5 to 3 hours. Each class is built on the previous one to some extent, with booster sessions held after the completion of the course. Needless to say, there can be many variations on this structure, but the main element is the gradual and systematic nature of the teachings and practice building. Immersion in a subject, as in reading a whole book quickly or attending an intensive retreat for a few days, has its own benefits. However, very often it does not result in sustained and regular practice, which is in the heart of the effectiveness of mindfulness and other meditative approaches.

Another important point to keep in mind is that novelty wears off. It is important to get introduced to new avenues of practice. It is equally important to practice them at some depth, past their novelty effect, before deciding to write them off as a consistent practice for you. The best practice is the one that you do every day. I will introduce new practices throughout the book, along with different ways in which you can be mindful. Keep your mind and heart open. Learn what is suggested, and practice it enough to get a real feel for it. You do not need to do every practice every day. Indeed, I encourage you to be selective. If you try a new method a few times and feel it is not for you, do not include it in your long-term practice plan. However, if you find every practice troublesome, you may want to persist longer and examine your thoughts, beliefs, motives, and feelings in greater depth.

Natural resistance in the form of boredom, negative thoughts, or judgmental attitude is a common response to new explorations such as mindfulness. Notice your resistance, and gently return to the practice you had set out to do. I emphasize, and will keep reminding you throughout the book, that the effectiveness of mindfulness depends on regular practice. No ifs, ands, or buts. Yoda, the small green wise man of the *Star Wars* movies, had it right when he said, "Try not! Do. Or DO NOT. There is no try."

Please also know that you can start over. Let go of self-criticism and self-judgment, and start over as many times as you need to. Recommit without holding the past against yourself. Past is gone. Future is not here. The present is the only moment you truly have and can work with. Commitment to practice and a kind and noncritical attitude about starting over are not mutually exclusive. They go to the heart of a mindful approach to life's experiences. Practice building requires your mindful attention and attitude of self-compassion.

One participant in my mindfulness class described his struggles with commitment to practice and the benefits of practice this way:

> It was last fall and things were particularly stressful with my school work and other work responsibilities. As often happens when my life gets really busy, my meditation practice falls to the wayside. But mindfulness is always in the back of my mind. It was kind of a dreary morning, raining lightly, and I was

45

transferring buses to go to work. I had been in a bad mood all morning. Nothing in particular had happened; I think it was just the constant feeling of stress. I was hurrying over to the next bus, looking down at the ground, wrapped up in my anxious thoughts, when I became aware of what was going on in my mind. I don't know where this shift came from, but once I was observing what was happening in my mind I just stopped walking. Standing there on the sidewalk I took a few deep, mindful breaths. I remember this next part pretty distinctly, because it was such a drastic shift. I looked up from the ground and the world looked brighter. I could have sworn that just a few seconds before it was a gray, overcast day, but now there was so much color. I remember the leaves on the trees in particular. They had already started to change colors as it was getting later in the season, and they looked so vibrant and rich. My mind had slowed too, and I could notice the feeling of the rain on my face, the cool air entering my lungs. But the most significant thing I noticed was my anxiety. It had disappeared. I had been so consumed with my thoughts just moments before, but after a few mindful breaths it was like I was living in a different world, internally and externally. My whole mood had changed, and this lasted for pretty much the rest of the day. It is moments like these that remind us how powerful mindfulness is, how beneficial it is in my life, and how important it is for me to practice.

WHAT YOU NEED TO START

To start, you need nothing. Even when you become an experienced practitioner, you will need nothing. In-between, however, as you read, learn, and experiment, I will advise you to build a simple but important infrastructure to support your practice. From my own experience and that of other teachers, practitioners, and class participants, I have found that without these supportive structures it is difficult to build a regular practice.

I have already outlined the importance of two elements of this infrastructure, a regular time and a private space—that is, a time when you will be alert, awake, and have enough energy to read and to experiment, and a place where you will feel safe and undisturbed. Please reread the section on making time and making a place if you have any doubts about the extent of their importance.

You will also need a notebook and a pen or a pencil. The notebook, or your practice journal, is a place to keep track of your experiences. Choose a notebook that you really like, or creatively personalize a simple one. Journaling in and of itself is an important source of mindful practice. It will help to articulate your experiences explicitly and keep track of the shifts and changes, which can enhance your consciousness and awareness about the work you are doing. With these four elements—time, place, paper, and pen—you can begin.

Soon (by the end of Lesson 2) you might find that you want a few more items. Following are some recommendations. If you decide to obtain some or all of these, get the ones that you like and can enjoy even in a small way. Get excited about your new project of mindfulness. Indulge a little without guilt and, of course, within your budget. Let the child in you come out and play. Playfulness, lightness, creatively, and joy are welcome now or anytime during your exploration and practice of mindfulness.

- *Yoga mat.* Yoga mats can facilitate exercises that are performed in lying-down positions and/or when yoga exercises are incorporated in weekly classes and daily practices. You can find yoga mats online, in sporting goods stores, and in some department stores. Pick a color that you like or a design that you enjoy. If you develop a successful practice, you might use this mat for a long time.

- *Cushion.* Cushions can help you sit comfortably on the floor or on a chair. You might want one to support a sitting meditation practice of increasing duration. I recommend taking your time before purchasing a cushion until you get to know how long of a sitting practice you would like to cultivate. Experiment with different styles, types, and sizes. The real objective here is comfortable sitting on the floor or on a chair. You may wish to purchase a *zafu.* These are specialized cloth seats for sitting meditation. They often are paired with *zabutons,* which are thick mats on which the zafu sits and are designed to protect your feet, ankles, and knees. Zafus and zabutons come in different sizes, heights, and fillings. There are also various small wooden stools (some of which are called *seiza benches*), with or without built-in cushions.

- *Timer or electric gong.* You will need a timer or an electric gong to announce the end of a practice session. Looking at your watch at brief intervals to see whether the time is up, especially in the early stages of practice development, is likely to disrupt the flow of your practice. Many timers have a rather abrupt sound. I prefer the soothing sound of an electric gong. You can find this online or in specialty stores. Some cell phones, computer programs, and websites can also provide you with the gong sound. In time and with experience, you will develop your internal timekeeper and will no longer need a gong. Until then, you will need a reliable manner of ending a practice.

- *Beginning and ending.* I recommend marking the start and end of each class and of your daily practice. A consistent way of beginning and ending the weekly class and daily practices helps to focus and center your attention. Think about a simple ritual that is meaningful for you. A statement or an activity can be helpful. I typically sit on my cushion in front of my altar, bring my hands together in the front my heart as in a prayer position, do a slight bow toward the altar, take a deep full breath, and silently say, "I am here." How you choose to start and end your class may be different from how you choose to begin and end your daily practice. Those with religious beliefs may start with a short prayer. Some light a candle or incense as a way of settling in. Burning incense and candles is a very popular form of adding ambiance to the place of practice. However, some research links the long-term use of incense to respiratory tract carcinomas (Friborg et al., 2008). Think about how you would like to begin. Similarly, a proper ending can help wrap up and smooth your transition to the next activity. Bowing, prayer, or dedication of the practice are among the possibilities. For example, my favorite dedication that we recite at the end of each class is as follows: "May any learning, understanding, or insight that came about today benefit us, benefit our loved ones, benefit your friends and colleagues, and may it ripple all the way out into the universe and benefit all beings."

- *Comfortable clothing.* For the weekly classes during which you work on the lessons from the book and your daily practices, always dress in loose fitting, comfortable clothing.
- *Blanket.* A soft, warm blanket will be very handy for lying-down or sitting practices.
- *Water.* Keep yourself hydrated at all times.

PRACTICE BUDDY

So far we have mentioned the importance of several elements including practice time and space, a sweet-sounding gong, and comfortable seating. Another very important factor in practice development is a supportive community. Small groups and major religions alike admit to the importance of a supportive, accepting, and loving community in practice development. This is an entire subject of discussion to itself.

For the moment and for the purpose of establishing your practice, try to identify a *practice buddy.* Your practice buddy could be a friend, a partner, a family member, or a coworker—preferably someone who cares about you, which would be an added bonus. The "caring" part is not essential. I have seen perfect strangers become wonderful practice buddies to each other. You will be shocked and amazed at how easily people agree to become your practice buddy if you only ask. Do not be surprised if they too become interested in what you are doing and decide to try.

The way it works is this: After you make your practice plan for the week, you declare it to your practice buddy either in person, in writing, or on the phone. Make sure that he or she understands what your plan is by having him or her repeat your plan to you. The role of the practice buddy, with agreed-on time and frequency of contact, is to express interest in your practice and to encourage your practice without badgering, giving advice, or making you feel bad in case of noncompliance. He or she should be someone with whom you feel comfortable talking about your practice. For example, the practice buddy can ask you one or more times during the week, "Are you on track with your practice?" If yes, great, describe what you have been doing. If no, then why? What is preventing you?

The practice buddy is yet another important practice reminder and one that creates an opportunity for you to voice how your practice is going. This will be a good source of information when you design your next practice plan. Your practice plan is a living and evolving document; it is never final. It is always the best it can be, always perfect and with room for improvement.

INTENTION TO EXPERIMENT, LEARN, AND PRACTICE

It may sound obvious, but it is crucial to have a clear intention to experiment, learn, and practice mindfulness if you want to develop a practice. We can easily become complacent and lose the clarity of our intention, in which case our practice will undoubtedly suffer. Your commitment to practice is a direct reflection of your intention. Making time, making a place, building the infrastructure for your practice, contacting your practice buddy, and journaling all rest on the clarity of your intention for practice. It will be helpful to state your intention out loud, to yourself, and to your buddy and write it down in your journal. Typically, you can start with an overarching intention and then make it specific to a given practice. Indeed, before starting each practice, you are invited to state your intention. For example, before beginning my practice I may say, "My intention for practice is to stay present to my life and cultivate peace. For today I intend to stay present to my breath for the next 30 minutes."

One of my class participants said the following:

> My intention is to learn and practice mindfulness. To do so, I intend to stay patient and curious about mindfulness. Today I like to pay special attention to judgmental thoughts. My intention is to notice whenever judgmental thoughts arise in my awareness during my practice of mindful walking.

USING A JOURNAL TO PLAN WEEKLY PRACTICE

To maximize the chances of regular practice, after each weekly lesson or daily practice, ask two simple questions and jot down your responses in your journal:

- What have I learned?
- What do I want to do with this learning?

In other words, how will you put this learning to use? What do you plan to do? See the Weekly Journal Example on the next page. Please remember that you can write as much as you want and in any style. The idea is to keep track of what you are planning to do and what you actually do.

Weekly Journal Example

Weekly Class, Wednesday, October 24

What did I learn?

I have learned how to mindfully breathe. I know that I can apply it formally and informally. Informally, I can do it anytime and anywhere. I may need to pick a sound or a visual reminder, "a practice bell" for informal practice. I have to think what mindfulness bell to use. To enhance the chances that I will develop a regular practice, I may need to choose a few gadgets, make time, create personal space, pick a practice buddy, and above all have a clear intention to learn and practice mindfulness.

What will I do with this learning?

- My intention is to learn and apply mindfulness to my life.
- I commit to regular practice of mindfulness for this week. I also commit to journaling and keeping track of my practice. More specifically, I will develop a practice plan for each day and then journal about how practice went for that day. The idea is to keep track of what I am planning to do and what I actually do.

Daily Practice Plan, Thursday, October 25

- I will do 5 minutes of mindful breathing in the morning after brushing my teeth.
- I will take two mindful breaths each time I look out of the window of my office.

(continues)

- I will pick my practice buddy.
- I will obtain a comfortable cushion and a timer or an electric gong for my sitting practice.
- I would like to read Lesson 1 of this book one more time to make sure that I remember important details.

Practice Review, Thursday, October 25

My informal practice included breathing mindfully five separate times today. I noted it had a resetting effect. I felt somewhat refreshed and relaxed afterward. I did mindful breathing for 5 minutes in the morning after I brushed my teeth. I used the kitchen timer. I felt its sound was a bit jarring. I would like something different to announce the end of my formal practice. I decided whom to ask to be my buddy. I have not contacted my buddy yet. I hope the person will accept. If not, I do have a couple of other people I can contact as a backup. I am a bit nervous that this person may say *no*. I am a little apprehensive about sharing something this personal. It is true that looking ahead can make one feel nervous! I stay in the moment for now without looking ahead. I found a cushion in the house to use. I was fine for the 5 minutes but can see that if I were to sit for 45 minutes, it could be uncomfortable. I looked ahead again! One day at a time for now. In any case, I can use a chair if need be. My mind wandered quite a bit, and I kept thinking how mindful breathing is going to work. I was able to catch myself thinking these thoughts and brought my mind back to the breathing. I think that is how it is and gradually my mind may wander less. I reread the book chapter. Picked up a few more points that I had missed. All in all I am excited and hopeful about incorporating mindfulness into my daily routines.

Daily Practice Plan, Friday, October 26
- 10 minutes of formal mindful breathing in the morning after brushing my teeth.
- Take two mindful breaths each time I look out of the window.
- 5 minutes of formal mindful breathing in the evening after I come home from work.
- Will contact my buddy to talk about my plan.

Practice Review, Friday, October 26

I breathed mindfully whenever I looked out of the window at home and at work. In the morning I was too rushed to do mindful breathing. I decided to do 15 minutes of formal mindful breathing in the evening. I reminded myself of my commitment. My mind kept wandering away either to the events of the day or to how tired I was. I kept coming back to the breath. I think the hardest part was to commit to doing it, and then it was not at all difficult to sit. Actually, I did feel more refreshed afterward. I contacted my buddy and talked about my plans. My buddy was agreeable, and we decided that my buddy will contact me once during the week by sending me an e-mail. We did not say which day of the week. We decided this could be variable.

Daily Practice Plan, Saturday, October 27
- 10 minutes of mindful breathing in the morning.
- 10 minutes of mindful breathing in the evening.

(continues)

- Take two mindful breaths each time I look out of the window.

Practice Review, Saturday, October 27

I have been getting used to breathing mindfully whenever I look out of the window of my office and home. Even when I see other windows I think of it and do it. No luck with morning mindful breathing, I woke up too late to do it. I did it for 15 minutes in the evening again. I might need to consider doing my formal practice in the evening rather than in the morning. I am going to hold out a bit longer and see. I think morning practice can start the day on the right note for me. Today I noticed that traffic lights are a good time to practice mindful breathing. I have been taking a few mindful breaths while waiting at the red lights. I will add this to my plan of informal mindfulness. So I have two mindfulness bells: windows and red lights.

Daily Practice Plan, Sunday, October 28

- Practice the same as today.
- Increase one of the sitting times to 15 minutes.
- Take two or more mindful breaths at traffic red lights.

Practice Review, Sunday, October 28

I did as I planned today. I do not like the sound of my kitchen timer and I have not yet done anything about it. I like to get something else. I will look on the Internet and will order one after I am done with journaling. In the meantime I will use the timer—and try to let go of my judgment about how it sounds! My buddy e-mailed me today asking how I am doing. It was nice to talk to someone about my practice.

II

CULTIVATING
ATTENTION

LESSON 1

MINDFUL BREATHING

This is your first weekly mindfulness class. Have you set aside time (1–2 hours) on a set day each week for your class? Is now your chosen time and day for the class? Are you in your safe and distraction-free space? Do you have pen and paper handy? Are you ready to fully engage in a short experiment? Have you decided on your preferred way, your personal ritual, for starting and ending your class?

When the answer to these questions is yes, you can begin. Throughout this book, each lesson follows the same basic structure. The first section, Start the Class, helps you establish your intention for the class. For all lessons after the first one, a subsequent section, Review Your Practice, will prompt you to consider how previous lessons are being integrated into your practice. The next section,

Class Reading, presents the conceptual information to build your practice—that is, the focus of that lesson—and guides you through a particular meditative practice. Finally, the Class Practice section prompts you to repeat this and previously discussed practices, write in your journal about the experience, and revise your practice plan as needed.

This first lesson is longer than future lessons, but it provides a necessary foundation. Mindful breathing is the most basic and important meditative practice.

START THE CLASS

- Perform your chosen start ritual.
- Take a few breaths, inhaling and exhaling fully and slowly.
- Gently close your eyes for a few moments and get in touch with the part of you that wants to learn and experiment with mindfulness. Come in touch with your intention to learn, to experiment, and to practice mindfulness. Silently state your intention.
- Then carefully read the following instructions.

CLASS READING

Chapter 3 and this lesson lay the foundation for the future lessons and provide detailed information. You may need to refer to these sections several times until you have become more familiar with the book format and practices.

Instructions for Mindful Breathing

Read the following instructions once through or as many times as you find necessary to feel at ease with them, and then try the exercise:

- *Establish good posture.* Bring attention to your posture. Sit upright and tall, with your spine erect but not stiff. Let your shoulders be relaxed and away from the ears. Open your chest. Tuck your chin slightly in. When sitting on a chair, the best approach is not to lean against the back of the chair, but rather to sit upright. The height of the chair will also matter. If your feet feel short compared with the height of the chair, put something under your feet. When sitting on the floor, the best approach is to sit cross-legged on a cushion. Sitting on a cushion helps support the back by keeping the spine straight and erect. Sometimes it helps to put additional support cushions under the knees. You may want to experiment until you find your optimum sitting position.

- *Relax your eyes.* You may keep your eyes closed or open. Many people keep their eyes gently closed. If you choose to keep your eyes open, maintain an unfocused, soft gaze 2 to 3 feet ahead.

- *Support your hands.* Rest your hands comfortably on your lap or knees. You may find that keeping your arms and elbows close to the body can help with the upright maintenance of your posture. Palms may be up or down. You may also rest one hand in the palm of the other.

- *Survey your body, mind, and heart.* Take notice of how it feels (tense, achy, soft, relaxed) in various parts of the body (feet, legs, torso, arms, hands, head, face), how it is in the mind (busy, wandering, focused), and how it feels in the heart (pleasant, unpleasant, neutral). Conduct a survey of how you are right now. There is no need to change anything. There is no right or wrong way to think, feel, or be right now. Just note what is present. Relax and, to the extent possible, let go of judgments, strivings, and expectations.

- *Attend to your breath.* Gently bring your attention to the breathing process. As you breathe in, notice that you are breathing in. And as you breathe out, notice that you are breathing out. Keep your attention and awareness on the breath. Attend to every detail of the inhalation and the exhalation. Note that as the air goes through the nostrils, down the windpipe, and down into the lungs, the belly expands while the lower part of the lungs fills up with air, then the belly contracts, goes back toward the spine, and the air comes out through the nostrils. Depending on your natural breathing habits, you may sense a subtle or a pronounced expansion of the belly or the chest. You do not need to manipulate your breath. Simply trace its natural flow with the mind's eye. The rhythm of the breath may shift during the exercise as well. Remain an observer.

- *Refocus your attention.* As you keep your attention on the breathing process, the mind will wander. When you notice the mind has wandered, silently acknowledge the wandering mind and gently bring the attention back to the breathing process without judgment. Each time, let go of what came before and allow the attention to the breath to be a new and fresh experience.

- *Have a compassionate attitude.* Bring forth and maintain a kind, gentle, accepting, and friendly attitude throughout the practice. Pay attention to each breath as if it were the first breath you have ever taken. No need to change anything. Stay attentive to the breathing process with gentle curiosity, friendliness, and receptivity. Notice the wandering mind and gently bring it back again and again to the inhalation and to the exhalation, without judgment or any particular expectation. There is no right or wrong way to do this. You may even smile as you practice paying attention to the breath. Smiling gives the body the message of ease, joy, and friendliness. Practice the focused attention on the breath for 5 minutes.

- *End the practice.* When the 5 minutes are up, gently open your eyes, and take note of how the body, the mind, and the heart feel. Take another general survey of how you are right now, briefly reflecting on your experience.

Interrelated Aspects of Mindfulness

When we practice mindfulness, we are cultivating several interrelated and overlapping features. In the previous exercise, we chose the breath as the anchor. The *anchor,* or the chosen area of the focus, can be any number of felt experiences, such as sight, sound, taste, smell, walking, eating, emotions, or thoughts. The following are what we actually are cultivating and strengthening during mindfulness:

- *Attention.* We attend to and become aware of the details of our felt experience as fully as possible. We see if it is a visual experience. We listen if it is a sound. We taste if it is food. We smell if it is a fragrance. Doing so, in time, sharpens our awareness and increasingly brings the habits of the mind under conscious control.

- *Present moment orientation.* Staying present and noticing when the mind wanders to the past or to the future is another important feature. We notice where the mind has gone to and then gently bring the attention back to the present moment as many times as necessary. In doing so, we are letting go of the past or the future. This trains the mind to stay present in the moment. A past orientation tends to contribute to dissatisfaction, sadness, and regret. A future orientation tends to contribute to anxiety and fear.

- *Nonjudgment.* We stay noncritical when the mind wanders. We do not expect a particular result. We notice when the mind becomes judgmental. We do not criticize the judgmental mind either. We simply note that the mind has become judgmental and return our attention back to the anchor. A noncritical attitude toward self and eventually others is cultivated during mindfulness.

- *Letting go.* By noticing the wandering mind, judgments, expectations, or any other thoughts, feelings, or sensations and bringing the attention back to the chosen anchor, we cultivate patience and the ability to let go. We may even smile during our practice, giving the body the message of ease and joy.

- *Beginner's mind.* By repeatedly bringing our attention back to the anchor and attending to it as if for the first time, we maintain an attitude of curiosity, openness, and wonder. This cultivates the ability to experience life in the moment with a fresh perspective rather than pass judgment on the basis of our previous experiences.
- *Acceptance.* We do not seek or expect any particular result. We accept our experience with openness, friendliness, and gratitude as it unfolds in each moment. This cultivates the ability to accept and engage in life fully.

Formal Practice

Mindfulness of the breath, and almost all mindfulness techniques, can be practiced formally or informally. A formal practice involves setting aside a certain time of the day for practice, usually between 20 minutes to 1 hour. Some traditions recommend practicing twice a day. Transcendental meditators meditate twice a day, 20 minutes each time (Rosenthal, 2011). It is important to decide how long and how often you want to practice mindful breathing. For the novice, it is best to begin with short periods and to increase the time as the practice strengthens and deepens. It is better to practice regularly (every day) for a short duration than to practice infrequently for a long period with less frequency. For example, 10 minutes of breath mindfulness per day is preferable to two 35-minute sessions per week.

Informal Practice

An informal practice is when we apply mindfulness and sprinkle it on various activities throughout the day. Informal practice of mindful breathing can be taking one or several mindful breaths throughout the day. One recommendation is to use something that occurs in the natural course of the day as an invitation to mindfulness. For example, sounds that regularly occur throughout the day can be used as reminders. Depending on your daily surroundings, such reminders can be household sounds, office sounds, nature sounds, etc. Pick a sound and use it as a signal to take one or two mindful breaths. Similarly, communication devices such as telephones and cell phones, as well as text message and e-mails, generally use sound as a signal. Before responding, take one or two mindful breaths.

There are also computer programs, websites, and cell phone applications that include mindfulness bells that can be easily programmed to desired frequencies with the pleasant sound of a gong (or other sounds). You may even pick an unavoidable sound in the environment that you find aversive as your mindfulness bell. Sirens and planes flying overhead could be examples. In time, these sounds will become just sounds without creating the same inner aversion or reactivity.

One also may use visual reminders. A friend and colleague of mine puts a small dot on his hand with a pen as a reminder. Each time during the course of the day he notices the dot, which is invisible to others, he takes a couple of mindful breaths. This same friend, in the process of building his practice of sitting meditation, used to put his zafu (meditation pillow) right by his bed. In the morning, he had to step on the zafu to get out of bed. The zafu in the morning provided a strong visual reminder of his desire to develop a sitting meditation practice. Other visual reminders could be a particular piece of jewelry, a certain color, or an article of clothing.

Regular activities are another rich source of reminders to be mindful. Each time you open or close a door, get in or out of the car, stop at a traffic light, before or after eating—the possibilities are endless. Feel free to experiment with this and other ideas and find something that can work for you as a reminder, your personal mindfulness bell, so that you will take mindful breaths during the day. Be selective—too many bells can become self-defeating.

Note the word *practice*. Whether it is formal or informal, practice implies engagement, involvement, and repetition. Learning mindfulness is like learning a musical instrument. It requires regular practice.

Commentary and Concluding Remarks

When we practice mindfulness, such as breath mindfulness, the purpose of the exercise is not to achieve a particular state. The purpose is to focus our attention and to become aware of our breath with all its exquisite intricacies. It is the habit of the mind to wander when we try to focus it on a single anchor. Notice the way your mind is working. This and similar exercises help steady the mind. Noticing internal experiences with a nonjudgmental, open-hearted awareness is the essence of mindfulness. There is no good or bad, better or worse, right or wrong. With practice, the mind becomes less judgmental. Remember, it is the mind's nature to judge, to wander, to go to the past or to the future. These functions are as natural to the mind as beating is to the heart or digestive contractions to the stomach.

Breath mindfulness is one of the most—if not the most—powerful, flexible, invisible, and seemingly simple ways to be mindful. The breath is ever present as long as we live. Breath mindfulness can be practiced for very brief periods or for a long time. It can be a few moments, several minutes, an hour, or longer. In some meditation retreats, mindfulness of the breath is used as the main teaching tool for several hours each day. In reality, there is no lower or upper time limits, and breath meditation can be done sitting, standing, or lying down.

Training in mindfulness is about self-healing and self-care. It promotes physical and emotional well-being. The practices are compassionate acts of self-care. Treat yourself with kindness in the process by holding no expectation of having a good time or any particular experience. Expectations can be a source of stress in themselves.

If you stop right here, read no further, and simply practice the mindfulness of the breath regularly, it could mean a lifetime of profoundly meaningful and transformative practice. Planning your practice in detail increases your chances of engagement. Whatever you committed to for your practice, say it out loud to yourself, write it down, and even sign the plan you wrote down. Hold it as if it is a commitment you have made to someone else. Don't you deserve the same consideration?

One participant in my mindfulness class poignantly described the importance of mindful breathing in a note that she sent me during a particularly rough period of her life 3 years later: "There is so much going on in all aspects of my life I can barely breathe. And mindful breathing is what usually keeps things sane and keeps me going."

CLASS PRACTICE

- *Set your timer/electric gong.* Set your timer for 5 minutes (or other time period).
- *Mindful breathing.* Perform mindful breathing as described previously.
- *Journal.* Journal about your experience. What did you notice? What did you notice about your breath? Was there anything different from usual? Did you discover anything that you did not know before? What else did you notice? Did your mind wander? What did the mind wander to? The past? The future? Did you note any judgments? Likes or dislikes? Bodily sensations? Emotions? In your efforts to attend to your breath, what else happened? Did you notice being bored, curious, relaxed . . . distracted? Fully describe your experience. Include all the details that you noticed. In short, what did you learn? Then explain what you will do with this learning. Plan your daily practice for the week. Refer to the Weekly Journal Example.
- *End of class.* Perform your chosen ritual to end the class before your next activity.

DISTINGUISHING THOUGHTS FROM AWARENESS

START THE CLASS

- Perform your start ritual.
- Take a few breaths, inhaling and exhaling fully and slowly.
- Gently close your eyes and come in touch with your intention to learn, experiment with, and practice mindfulness.
- Open your eyes and continue reading.

REVIEW YOUR PRACTICE

- Are you in your class location right now?
- Is it the day, time, and place to which you have committed?
- Do you feel safe and at home in your practice place?

- Do you have clear intentions to learn, explore, and practice mindfulness?
- Do you have your journal?
- Have you personalized it in any way?
- Have you been practicing mindful breathing?
- Do you have a practice buddy?
- Are you clear about your start and ending rituals for the class and your daily practices?

If the answer to the previous questions is yes, continue with the following readings. If not, it is crucial to pause and ask yourself a few questions. For a growing practice, it is necessary to be realistic. I recommend that you reread this chapter several times in the next few weeks, especially when you feel that your practice is not on the right track. The following questions can help you sort out what works, what doesn't, and how you can make modifications:

- Are the initial day, time, and place of your practice working? If not, which one is not working? What changes do you need to make to "attend" your class on time?
- How about your daily practice plan? Have you followed your plan? If not, did you over- or underestimate? Do you want to add to or subtract from your plan to make it workable and meaningful?
- Have you had any contact with your buddy? If not, what are the issues, and how can they be addressed? Is there another way you can establish a sense of community during mindfulness training?
- Are you excited or discouraged or . . . ?

Whatever the thoughts and emotions regarding the practice, I encourage you to choose to stay side by side with these or other thoughts and emotions that may come up without either giving up or developing high expectations. All emotions and thoughts are welcome. Consider them as welcomed guests that come and that go. They are not the boss that you have to obey or take orders from. It is not thoughts or emotions in themselves but the way in which we relate to them that makes a difference. Relate to them as a guest and not as a boss. Remember, guests are impermanent. Accept them as they are. Be nice to them whether you approve or not. Mindfully breathe along with them and notice what unfolds. Thoughts and emotions shift constantly throughout the day. The University of California, Los Angeles, Laboratory of Neuroimaging's Brain Trivia website (http://www.loni.ucla.edu/About_Loni/education/brain_trivia.shtml) puts the estimate of the number of thoughts we have during each day at 70,000. We probably have an equal or larger number of emotions going through us each day as well, given that each thought can generate more than one emotion.

As you read the previous lines, take note of your thoughts about your practice right now. Are you curious, excited, neutral, or engaged in self-defeating thoughts? Are you making excuses in your mind for not following through? Are you skeptical, belittling, or undermining your own efforts? Are you overzealous or expecting immediate results? What are the self-talks that might be influencing you right now? Bring to mind thoughts that have influenced your practice during the past week.

CLASS READING

Thought and Awareness

Now is a great time to begin separating your thoughts and emotions from your actions. The mindful approach distinguishes between thinking and awareness. In this approach, we observe thoughts and emotions kindly and lovingly and continue with our planned practice, which will strengthen the capacity to witness thoughts and related emotions without reactivity. Jack Kornfield (2008), in his book *The Wise Heart*, defined mindfulness as nonjudgmental and respectful attention and the ability to distinguish awareness from mental activity. He stated that to learn mindfulness is to learn to be aware of our own mental states without being caught in them. This is a very important concept. It is about the distinction between the thoughts that go through the mind (e.g., thoughts of the past or future, judgments about what we are feeling or sensing) and our pure awareness of those thoughts. Our thoughts come and go, but the awareness that notices those thoughts is not the thoughts themselves. This awareness is that unvarying part of our consciousness that has been here throughout time, from the moment we can remember ourselves (i.e., from childhood) to the present moment. It is the awareness that knows the "I" from 2 minutes ago, an hour ago, a year ago, 10 years ago and that can even project into the future. It is the consciousness that knows the "I" in spite of all the personal changes and the passage of time, the awareness that experiences thoughts, sensations, and feelings but itself is none of these. The "I" cannot be seen yet is the essence of the person. Ken Wilber (2007), writer and philosopher, called it the *I Amness*.

In reality, the physical body goes through continual changes as it evolves, matures, and decays. The cells are constantly dying and being replaced by new ones. The tissues with which life began all die within the first few years of life. In effect, one has a new physical body every few years. Yet, there is that sense of "I" that never changes and stays constant beyond the changing nature of the physical form.

Initially, the awareness that can observe and witness experience without entanglement can be quite slippery, difficult to identify and maintain. It becomes more accessible as the muscles of mindfulness grow and strengthen. The observer becomes more present and pronounced with persistent practice. This transformation, the observer that experiences without entanglement, can eventually free us from the volatile grip of reactivity. We gradually develop an accepting relationship with our thoughts and feelings. We stand side by side with various thoughts and emotions without an urgent need to act or react.

It is important to note that "not getting caught" in emotional reactivity and letting go of thoughts, emotions, and sensations is not the same as dissociating from our experience, pushing them away, turning away, or suppressing them. It is far from it. Not getting caught and letting go is really about letting be. It is about acknowledging the presence of all kinds of thoughts, emotions, and sensations and yet developing the ability to witness them without inner or outer reactivity. It is to be with them and stand along with them with acceptance.

Remind yourself that thoughts and emotions are passing phenomena. You need not avoid or attach to them. Let your thoughts come and go without equating them with the truth or with who you are. You do not have to believe your thoughts. You can choose to allow your actions to be influenced by them or to let them go. Thinking is a part of our being similar to breathing. Thoughts are an aspect of our human condition. Thoughts are neither our controller nor our enemy. They are a natural part of having our human brains. The same way our heart beats or our stomach digests, our brain thinks. We need not battle our thoughts, nor do we need to let them run our mind and our behavior. Our mind is capable of witnessing thoughts without getting caught in them. Befriend your thoughts without attachment; understand them, let them be, let them come, and let them go. Notice their strength, persistence, and content without getting caught in the story they tell. You are not your thoughts. The same goes for the emotions that bring them about, accompany them, or come after them. Befriend your emotions as well. Separating the mind from thoughts that go through the mind, from the sensations in the body, and from emotions that we feel can help us strengthen our ability to stand side by side with thoughts, feelings, and sensations with receptivity.

As a novice, you will begin strengthening this witness, the observing quality of your mind, your unencumbered awareness, with manageable and not very strong or persistent thoughts, sensations, and emotions. Mindful exploration of thoughts and emotions related to your first week of practice can be a good place to start. Consistent practice will enable you to witness even strong emotions and persistent thoughts mindfully with receptivity and without getting caught in them.

Practice Plan Revisited

If you need to make major revisions to your plan, stop here. Go back to Chapter 3 and Lesson 1. Review them one more time and make needed modifications to your plan on the basis of the information you have now collected about yourself and your practice. Decide if you would like to reorganize your practice or if you prefer to try again and recommit to the same plan one more time. When making changes to your initial plan or if you decide to try again, do so without self-criticism or judgment. Note any thoughts of defeat, failure, shame, inadequacy, irritation, blame, or trivializing the work itself. Note all these thoughts without being caught in the story or letting such thoughts discourage your planning. These thoughts may come in small doses. Try to catch them early and even in their mild forms. Take note of your experience and attend to even mild thoughts or feelings right now. What thoughts are going through your mind regarding modifying your plan, trying again, or reworking Chapter 3 and Lesson 1? Mindful exploration of your thoughts and emotions about your practice can help with mindful exploration of thoughts and feelings in general.

In planning your practice, become aware of the tendency to overdo it. More is not always better. Behind the idea of *more is better* may lie unrealistic expectations or competitiveness—an attitude of *getting there faster*. In the practice of mindfulness, you probably are beginning to note that there is no "other" place to get to. Speed is irrelevant. The grass on the other side is not greener. In his book *Peace is Every Step*, Thich Nhat Hanh (1992b) said that the miracle is not to walk on water. The miracle is to walk on the green earth, dwelling deeply in the present moment and feeling truly alive. The practice is to stay here in this moment—in the *now*. Efficiency can take on a completely new meaning in this context; it is to slow down and to pay full attention to yourself—to your breath, sensations, thoughts, and emotions—and to gently, attentively, and fully experience what is here.

Experiment

Choosing what to do about your practice while allowing various thoughts and emotions to coexist can be the most mindful practice available to you in the present moment. Take full advantage of this experience. You may think and feel that this is hard, irrelevant, ridiculous, uncomfortable, or wonderful, amazing, fantastic, or boring. Get the *witness,* the *observer,* on board—that part of your awareness that notices without being entangled. Remind yourself that all such thoughts are only guests, not the boss.

Right now, take several mindful breaths. Witness the thoughts and emotions that might have been stirred up in response to reading these pages about your practice. Close your eyes for a couple of minutes and reflect on the thoughts and emotions that are going through you right now. Have the witness, the "I," stand side by side with the thoughts and emotions. *I see you thoughts and emotions, welcome whatever you are.*

Sometimes it is useful to label each thought or emotion as you are witnessing it. Try to label the thoughts and emotions that are going through you. Labeling in this stage of practice development can strengthen the capacity to be mindful. For example, you might think, "I have always bought self-help books and never followed through. I probably will not do it this time either, or I feel so guilty that I did not follow through with my practice. I am hopeless, or I know this stuff and do I not think this is helpful." Such thoughts could be labeled as *judgmental*. There may be past thoughts or future thoughts. When you note such thoughts and become mindful of them in your awareness, you could say something like "Ah, I notice judgmental thoughts," or "Self-defeating thoughts are here. I see you. You show up each time I want to do something new," or "You show up whenever I am tired—I know you, my old friend," or "I am thinking in the future or in the past." Gently let go of the thoughts and return your attention to the present moment.

Practice Is Not Perfect

In Japanese culture and art, there is a concept of beauty called *wabi-sabi*. Unlike the Greek ideal of beauty, which relies on perfection and has influenced the West for centuries, wabi-sabi sees beauty in what is imperfect, impermanent, and incomplete. It is an acknowledgment that nothing lasts, nothing is finished, and nothing is ever perfect. Rumi, the Persian poet, mystic, and philosopher who lived 800 years ago, stated the same idea in one of his poems and said that it is through our wounds that the "light" gets inside our being. Leonard Cohen, a Canadian singer, songwriter, musician, poet, and writer, recaptured this sentiment in his song "Anthem." He said there is a crack in everything and that is how the light gets in. What makes us vulnerable and imperfect is exactly what makes us beautiful, magnificent, and human. As we talk about cultivating practice in a nonjudgmental way, I would like to emphasize that imperfection is part of the process. Indeed, in imperfection and struggle you will find the beauty of a growing practice that will never be perfect. In that process, you will discover the nuances of your own being, the ways in which your mind and heart work—the ever-changing mind and heart for which the concept of perfection is meaningless. Or rather, everything is perfect as it is.

CLASS PRACTICE

- *Breath mindfulness.* Now practice 10 minutes of breath mindfulness. Refer to the mindfulness of the breath instructions in Lesson 1 if you need to.

- *Journal.* It will be useful for you to journal about your experience right now. As you journal, you will see that certain thoughts and emotions regarding your practice may repeat themselves before you become an expert in "noticing" them. By journaling and putting them in writing, it will be easier for you to strengthen and further develop the capacity to witness thoughts and emotions. The capacity to witness without entanglement is the key to developing mindfulness. In addition, as you learn various techniques, your journal can be the source of your practice selection as you return to it to see what worked and what did not work. Journaling can be an effective tool in illuminating your practice path. Ask two questions: What have I learned from this lesson? How would I put it into practice? Be sure to make a plan of practice for the week. Use the wisdom you have gained from the first week to develop a plan for the second week of your practice.

- *End of class.* Perform your chosen ritual to end the class.

BODY SCAN

START THE CLASS

- Perform your start ritual.
- Take a few breaths, inhaling and exhaling fully and slowly.
- Gently close your eyes and come in touch with your intention to learn, experiment with, and practice mindfulness.
- Open your eyes and continue reading.

REVIEW YOUR PRACTICE

How is your practice going? Have you been in contact with your practice buddy? Have you been practicing mindful breathing? Are you generally satisfied with your practice? If not, review Lesson 2. If yes, continue reading.

CLASS READING

Mindfulness of the Body

Becoming mindful of the body and bodily sensations is an important step in cultivating mindfulness. The number of ways in which we can become aware of our body and its sensations are unlimited. Body scan, progressive muscle relaxation, synchronization of various movements and yoga poses with the breath, mindful standing, mindful walking, tai chi, qigong, exercise, and massage can be considered effective ways to become mindful of the body. Addressing all the possibilities is beyond the scope of this book. However, I will highlight several that I believe to be useful considerations for both the beginner and the experienced practitioner alike. We will learn body scan, progressive muscle relaxation, mindful standing and walking, and mindful movements in this and future lessons. If you already have an effective form of practice in this domain, continue with your practice and apply what you have learned about mindfulness to your existing activity. For example, long-time yoga practitioners often discover a vast new frontier when they apply mindfulness to yoga. Learning new practices does not necessitate giving up what is already working for you.

In my mindfulness class, one participant with a great interest in golf found out that she played her best games when she applied mindfulness. Another participant, an avid runner, described his integration of mindfulness into his running practice this way:

> I had heard but did not really understand what it meant when some other runners talked about focusing on the body during running. Since learning about mindfulness in the past three

weeks, I decided to apply it to running. I have now been focusing my attention on my body sensations and movement during running. I religiously measure all aspects of my body physiology during running. With initial disbelief, I have noted that I can reduce my heartbeat by five beats per minute when I run mindfully. This is a breakthrough for me!

Body Scan

The *body scan* is a process by which the focus of attention is systematically brought to various parts of the body to increase awareness of existing bodily sensations. The purpose is neither to relax nor to feel good. You do not need to change anything. The task is to direct mindful attention to each body part, bringing that part into sharp focus and taking note of the sensations that are present.

Similar to breath mindfulness, during the body scan, the loving and friendly attitude of acceptance, nonjudgment, and the beginner's mind is engaged—noticing, allowing, accepting, and when the mind wanders, refocusing. The sensations you will discover may be experienced as pleasant, unpleasant, or neutral. Try to become aware of any tendency to recoil or attach to any of the sensations you discover. The idea is to be an unbiased observer of your body's sensations.

Read the following instructions carefully, and when you are ready, you can practice the body scan. Most mindfulness instructors recommend lying down. I recommend lying down for initial learning. After you have gained sufficient familiarity and skill with the technique, you can practice it sitting or even standing if necessary.

- *Take care of logistics.* You will need a quiet place. You might also want a yoga mat or light blanket to lie down on, as well as a pillow or rolled-up towel to put under your knees (sometimes pressure on the lower back is released if you put a pillow or rolled-up towel under the knees).

- *Get comfortable.* Arrange yourself comfortably on the floor.
- *Focus inward.* Bring the attention toward yourself—the inner space. Gently breathe into your abdomen on the inhalation and then allow a complete exhalation. Inhale and exhale through the nose. Allow the eyes to close. Quiet the mind with a few mindful breaths.
- *Establish your intention.* Acknowledge your intention for the practice you are about to do. For example, your intention could be to stay fully attentive and present during the practice. Come up with a phrase that captures your intention and say it out loud or silently.
- *Take inventory.* Bring the attention to the body for a general survey. Take note of the quality of your mind, heart, and body. Simply notice what is present without trying to change anything. Think of yourself as the explorer, the discoverer of all of your body's various sensations. Following are a few examples, but do not limit yourself to these: notice the sensations associated with the places on your body that are in contact with the floor/mat, or if sitting, with the seat; notice the parts of your body that are in contact with the air; and notice the sensation of cloth on the skin.
- *Notice individual sensations.* After the general survey, bring your attention to specific body parts and take notice of sensations in each of them, one by one. Try to stay on each

sensation long enough to investigate what is happening there. Notice pressure, tension, warmth, cold, itchiness, pain, or any other sensations that are present. Sometimes you may feel nothing when surveying a certain body part. Notice that too. You may consider the following sequence. First, turn your attention to the left foot—toes, sole, heel, top of the foot, ankle, calf and shin, knee, thigh. Then to the right foot—toes, sole, top, heel, ankle, calf and shin, knee, thigh. Then to the entire pelvic region, buttocks, hips, genitals. Then to the lower back, abdomen, lungs, heart region, mid chest, mid back, upper back, shoulders, right side of the neck, front of the neck, back of the neck, left side of the neck, back of the head, top of the head. Then to the facial area—forehead, temples, eyes, eyebrows, muscles around the eyes, jaw, mouth, nose, muscles around the nose, and tongue. Stay present to, and keep your attention on each part long enough to know what is happening in that part of the body.

- *Witness your thoughts and feelings.* During the body scan, notice your thoughts, judgments, and emotional tone. Are you lingering when you find a sensation pleasant? Or recoiling if it feels unpleasant? Try to remain nonjudgmental. Congratulate yourself when you become mindful of your judgments and then let go of the judgment consciously. Engage your capacity to witness and observe the sensations that are present without getting tangled in them. Maintain an attitude of acceptance. You may discover sensations that you were not aware of. Allow all sensations that are here to be here without attachment. Turning toward, or recoiling from, are the two sides of the coin of attachment.

- *Connect to your breath.* Stay connected to your breath during the exercise. One way to remain connected to your breath is to let go of one body part when you exhale and, with your next inhalation, to bring the attention to another body part.

- *End.* After completing the body scan, bring your attention back to the breath and continue with a few mindful breaths, gently moving your arms and legs and bringing your consciousness back to your surroundings.

Incorporating the Body Scan Into Your Practice

Now you can add the body scan to your practice. This practice could be done for a brief or a long period of time. In the beginning, take your time and become familiar with every part of your body and its sensations. If not daily, consider incorporating the body scan into your practice two to three times per week.

If incorporated as a formal practice, the body scan commonly takes from 15 to 45 minutes or even up to 1 hour to perform. There are many tapes and CDs on the market with anywhere from 15 to 45 minutes of instructions. With repeated practice, even a 5- to 10-minute regular body scan can enhance mindfulness effectively. Some practitioners find this relaxing and do it regularly. Informal practice of the body scan can be done anywhere and in any position.

One participant in my mindfulness class, a chronic insomniac, applied the body scan at bedtime. She shared with the class that she now does a body scan every night. She has prosthetic hips that cause her discomfort particularly at night around bedtime. She stated that she knows the purpose of this exercise is to become more mindful of her body, body parts, and their various sensations and not necessarily to fall asleep. She also said that every time she performs the body scan and accepts the discomfort she has in her hips, she eventually becomes so relaxed that she falls asleep before the body scan is finished.

CLASS PRACTICE

- *Body scan.* Perform the body scan as previously described.
- *Mindful breathing.* Perform 15 minutes of mindful breathing.
- *Journal.* What did you notice? Describe your experience in detail. What did you learn from this lesson? What do you want to do with this learning? Decide how you want to incorporate the body scan into your weekly practice.
- *End of class.* Perform your chosen ritual to end the class.

PROGRESSIVE MUSCLE RELAXATION

START THE CLASS

- Perform your start ritual.
- Take a few breaths, inhaling and exhaling fully and slowly.
- Gently close your eyes and come in touch with your intention to learn, experiment with, and practice mindfulness.
- Open your eyes and continue reading.

REVIEW YOUR PRACTICE

How is your practice going? Have you been in contact with your practice buddy? Have you been practicing mindful breathing and the body scan? Are you generally satisfied with your practice? If not, review Lesson 2. If yes, continue reading.

CLASS READING

The body scan is an effective way to become aware of the body. Another effective practice that can increase awareness of the body is systematic tensing and relaxing of various muscle groups or *progressive muscle relaxation*. This procedure can vary along several dimensions, including the muscle groups, the sequence of muscle groups, the duration of tension periods, and the duration of relaxation periods. This method was first popularized in the West by Edmund Jacobson (1929), a well-known Harvard professor and physician, and has been modified over the years. A diverse and positive array of psychological, cognitive, emotional, physiological, and behavioral results have been attributed to this technique (Bernstein, Borkovec, & Hazlett-Stevens, 2000). Some prominent yoga practitioners have incorporated tension–relaxation into their teachings. For example, Paramahasana Yogananda, the renowned yogi and guru, used muscle tension–relaxation in his teachings. It is likely that he incorporated this technique on the basis of the teachings that he received in India before coming to the United States.

The main idea in this technique is to focus the attention on both sensations of tension and then relaxation and to systematically engage various major muscle groups to enhance the awareness of both muscle tension and relaxation. With repeated practice and consistent use, the practitioner learns to identify even small amounts of tension in various muscles and becomes able to consciously relax tense muscles.

This section represents one approach among an unlimited number of combinations and possibilities. It is customary to do the practice lying down. It could also be modified for a sitting or even standing position.

- *Breathe.* Bring your attention to the inner space and take several deep and mindful breaths.
- *Establish your intention.* Silently acknowledge your practice intention.
- *Survey your body.* Lie down comfortably. Bring the attention to the breathing process, and then gently conduct a survey of the body. There is no need to change anything; simply notice the sensations that are currently present.
- *Stretch.* With each stretch, hold for about three breaths before releasing.
  1. Stretch your body by pointing your toes toward one wall and putting your arms behind your head and stretching your fingers toward the opposite wall. Make your body as long as possible without straining. The feet can be stretched by pointing both the toes and/or the heels. After a complete stretch, release the stretch.
  2. Stretch your right arm and right leg. Release.
  3. Stretch your left arm and left leg. Release.
  4. Stretch your right arm and left leg. Release.
  5. Stretch your left arm and right leg. Release.
- *Tense and relax various muscle groups.* Tense and relax various muscle groups in the recommended order. It is important to harmonize your breaths with this activity. With the inhalation, tighten the specific muscle group and maintain the tension for a few seconds while remaining

fully attentive to the sensation of tension. With the exhalation, quickly release the muscle group and fully attend to the sensation of relaxation for a few seconds. Inhale and exhale through the nose. You may consider the following order of tension–relaxation: feet, calves, thighs, hips/buttocks, abdomen/stomach, lower back, chest, upper back, shoulders, hands and fingers, forearms, upper arms, neck (right, back, front, and left sides), eyes and the muscles around the eyes, mouth, and forehead.

- *Tense and relax your whole body.* After the systematic tensing and relaxing of the individual muscles, you may tense and relax the entire body. To do so, bring your arms to your sides and your feet together. Lift the feet and arms a couple of inches off the floor while your head is still resting on the ground. Now create tension in your entire body, tightening all the muscles you worked with individually for a few seconds and then relax the body. You may repeat this three times, with a few seconds of rest in-between. Over time you may increase the whole body tension from a few seconds to a period of 1 minute.

- *Rest.* Now rest for a few minutes and allow your breath to become natural. Allow the weight of your whole body to be supported by the ground under you. Consciously keep each muscle in a relaxed state, if possible. Take note of sensations that are present. Take note of the muscles that are readily relaxing and those that are not. If you choose to do this activity regularly, you will notice the shifts that will occur in your ability to relax your body.

Progressive muscle relaxation can be a wonderful way to release stress and at the same time become more aware of the body and bodily sensations, especially stress-related bodily sensations. I have seen and personally experienced the desire to fully relax posttension–relaxation. A brief rest period of 1 to 5 minutes is sufficient, and then you can continue with breath mindfulness. Progressive muscle relaxation can be done effectively in 10 minutes. One can feel refreshed and energized. This is a versatile technique and can be incorporated in a variety of ways, such as before a sitting practice or body scan, or any time during the day when you are feeling tension or fatigue in the body.

CLASS PRACTICE

- *Body scan.* Perform a short, 5-minute body scan.
- *Progressive muscle relaxation.* Perform progressive muscle relaxation as described previously.
- *Body scan.* Perform another short body scan.
- *Breath mindfulness.* Perform 15 minutes of breath mindfulness.
- *Journal.* Describe your experience in detail, especially your experience with progressive muscle relaxation. What did you notice? What did you learn from this lesson? What will you do with this learning? You can now incorporate breath mindfulness, a body scan, and progressive muscle relaxation in your daily practice. You may combine progressive muscle relaxation with a body scan. Personally, I prefer to perform a short body scan, followed by progressive muscle relaxation, then followed by another short body scan.
- *End of class.* Perform your chosen ritual to end the class.

MINDFUL STANDING AND WALKING

START THE CLASS

- Perform your start ritual.
- Take a few breaths, inhaling and exhaling fully and slowly.
- Gently close your eyes and come in touch with your intention to learn, experiment with, and practice mindfulness.
- Open your eyes and continue reading.

REVIEW YOUR PRACTICE

How is your practice going? Have you been in contact with your practice buddy? Have you been practicing mindful breathing, the body scan, and progressive muscle relaxation? Are you generally satisfied with your practice? If not, review Lesson 2. If yes, continue reading.

CLASS READING

Mindful Standing

Standing mindfully is a simple and versatile practice. It enhances body awareness, balancing, and centering. It is typically incorporated as an introduction to other forms of mindful movements, such as mindful walking or yoga.

- *Get in a good standing position.* Stand straight, with your feet firmly on the ground, spine straight, neck balanced on the shoulders, chin slightly tucked in, shoulders relaxed and away from the ears, and knees soft and unlocked.
- *Close your eyes, and establish your intention.* Breathing deeply and fully, clarify your intention for this practice and the duration of the practice. The intention can be to stay present, engage fully, remain curious, keep an open and non-judgmental mind, or any other statement of intention that is meaningful to you.
- *Attend.* Bring your full attention to the standing position. Stand as if you were growing roots at one end and attached by a thread from the head to the ceiling (or sky) at the other end.
- *Sense.* Note the sensations at the bottom of your feet. Note how you are balanced. Note the four corners of your feet: heel, ball, and sides. Stand motionless while becoming aware of the muscles that are keeping your body upright. Note that you are not, in fact, motionless! There are a host of micromovements that are keeping you upright.

The next two steps can be practiced for added vigor:

- *Move.* Gradually exaggerate these micromovements by swaying from side to side. Inhale to the right, exhale to the left. The arms will be making circles around you. Eventually engage the legs and the hips for about 1 minute. Then gently begin to make smaller and smaller movements and come to stillness.
- *Reverse.* Inhale to the left, exhale to the right. Eventually engage the legs and the hips for about 1 minute. Begin to make smaller and smaller movements slowly, and then come to stillness.
- *End.* Become aware of the breath, heartbeat, feet, legs, knees, arms, back, shoulders, hands, and head. Do a general survey of the body. Notice all of the sensations that are present. Gently end the practice and bring your attention back to your current surroundings.

Mindful Walking

Thich Nhat Hanh (1992b), in his well-known book *Peace Is Every Step,* stated that walking meditation is really to enjoy the walking—not in order to arrive, but just to walk. The purpose is to be in the present moment. He said walk as if you are kissing the Earth with your feet. He emphasized the importance of gratitude and joy for each step we take and reminded us that whenever we walk, we are not only walking for ourselves but also for those who cannot walk because of either disability or old age. He encouraged the awareness of surroundings and attention to nature, people, and scenery when walking.

Walking is another daily activity to which we can bring our mindful attention. It is used extensively in mindfulness or other forms of meditative retreats to alternate with sitting meditation. It can be done as a part of a formal practice, or it can be done informally, anytime and anywhere. It can be practiced indoors or outdoors. Typically, you slow down to practice mindful walking. However, you may want to stay mindful even when you walk at your normal speed or you walk fast or run for exercise. One way to become more aware and mindful of walking is to experiment with your habitual ways of walking and change them in some way. You can even bring in humor and practice walking sideways or backwards. Instructions for mindful walking are as follows:

- *Step.* In the classic form of mindful walking, you slow down and bring your mindful attention to the basic elements of a step.
  1. Lift one foot.
  2. Move the lifted foot forward.
  3. Place that foot on the ground.
  4. Then as you shift your weight to that foot, begin the lifting process with the other foot.

  You can parse the elements of a step even further by focusing on the various parts of your foot itself. In this case, the elements of a step are right foot (heel, ball, toes), left foot (heel, ball, toes), right foot (heel, ball, toes), left foot (heel, ball, toes), etc. In mindful walking we practice awareness of these different components of each step. Note the manner in which you shift your weight in the process. There are limitless ways in which a step is experienced. In the same way that no two breaths are exactly alike, no two steps are exactly alike.

- *Connect to the breath.* Do not lose your connection to the breath during mindful walking. You can incorporate walking with the rhythm of your breath for enhanced consciousness of both walking and the breath.
- *Sense.* Notice the bodily sensations in each component of the step.
- *Hands.* You can clasp your hands in front of the body, put one hand in the other, or hold your hands together in the back. Some people feel distracted by the movement of their arms when hands are not held together during mindful walking.
- *Refocus.* When the mind wanders or judgments, emotions, or thoughts arise, acknowledge them and gently bring the attention back to walking.

Many people who struggle with sitting meditations use mindful walking as a gateway to a sitting meditation practice. In my mindfulness class, one participant said:

> I have been having a lot of difficulty sitting with my breath. I feel restless and my mind wanders. Sitting is frustrating for me. But I can walk mindfully. I can keep my mind on the walking. I actually enjoy it. Now, I first walk for about 15 minutes and then sit for 10 minutes while focusing on mindful breathing. I

can do both with ease. The occasional frustration is not very strong, and I can observe it without stopping my practice. I know breathing is not the cause of my frustration! I am trying to understand my frustrations better. I think I become restless because I jump ahead in my thoughts and become anxious about all the things I have to do. Then judgmental thoughts come in, such as: "With all you need to do, it is stupid to sit here and watch your breath." Then I let go of the thoughts and bring my attention to the present. The more I keep my mind in the now, the easier it is to sit.

CLASS PRACTICE

- *Body scan and progressive muscle relaxation.* Perform a short body scan followed by progressive muscle relaxation and then another short body scan.
- *Breath mindfulness.* Perform 15 to 30 minutes of sitting breath mindfulness.
- *Mindful standing and walking.* Perform mindful standing as described previously, followed by mindful walking for 15 to 30 minutes.
- *Journal.* Describe your experience of mindful standing and walking in detail. What did you learn? What will you do with this learning? How will you incorporate it into your practice? Mindful standing and walking are very versatile and can be incorporated informally in regular daily activities. For example, take a mindful breath and stand mindfully for 15 seconds to 1 minute, taking note of bodily sensations head to toe each time you open or close a door. This seemingly simple informal practice can become a pow-

erful way to be mindful throughout the day and to incorporate three different mindful practices (breath, body scan, standing) regularly. Or take a number of steps in a mindful manner each day. Even 10 or 20 steps throughout the day will keep you in touch with a mindful approach to walking.

- *End of class.* Perform your chosen ritual to end the class.

LESSON 6

MINDFUL MOVEMENTS AND YOGA

START THE CLASS

- Perform your start ritual.
- Take a few breaths, inhaling and exhaling fully and slowly.
- Gently close your eyes and come in touch with your intention to learn, experiment with, and practice mindfulness.
- Open your eyes and continue reading.

REVIEW YOUR PRACTICE

How is your practice going? Have you been in contact with your practice buddy? Have you been practicing mindful breathing, body scan, progressive muscle relaxation, mindful standing, and mindful walking? Are you generally satisfied with your practice?

If not, what modifications do you need to make? You may also review Lesson 2.

CLASS READING

Many types of movements, including yoga, tai chi, and qigong poses, can be practiced mindfully in harmony with the breath to create a sequence of movements that tone, energize, and relax the body; increase vitality and awareness; and facilitate meditative practice. I know practitioners who have even included various dance forms in their practice. The essential components are the same: movement, harmonizing the movement and the breath, and enjoying or cultivating a sense of joy in the process. Sometimes the joy comes only after the completion of the activity!

The number of postures, poses, and sequences is limitless. For example, there are 20 or more different schools of yoga. Each prescribes and teaches a different set of movements consistent with its broader philosophy, perspective, and emphasis. The practices use the various body postures and movements as a part of a larger practice to harmonize and unite the body, mind, and spirit. The body is viewed as the "temple" of the spirit by all of the various schools. In its larger context, yoga includes nutrition, movement and exercise, rest, meditation, and a positive and loving attitude toward self and others (Ramacharaka, 1931).

What is most commonly known in the West as *yoga* is largely the hatha yoga body postures or *asanas*. Hatha yoga is very diverse and includes methods such as Ashtanga and Iyengar. Kundalini yoga is another popular form of yoga. Iyengar focuses on body alignment.

Ashtanga is dynamic and more aerobic. Kundalini focuses on the body's energy centers known as *chakras* and movement of energy in the body. All forms of yoga encourage conscious breathing and coordination of breath with movement. They also encourage stretching without strain or pain, pushing physical limits and endurance without going beyond limits (Becker, 2000; Bushell, 2009; S. K. Khalsa, 2001; S. P. K. Khalsa, 1966; Leonard & Murphy, 1995; Mehta, 1994; Olivo, 2009; Raman, 1998; Schiffmann, 1996; Sivananda Yoga Center, 2000; Vishnu-Devananda, 1988).

Viewing various forms of yoga or other practices can help you pinpoint what you may like best. After viewing several yoga practices, you can begin to note the quality of the teachings and movements. This can help you with the preliminary decision about which kind of movements better meet your body, mind, and spiritual needs. Note that your decision may change over time, and you can adjust your choices as your body becomes more flexible. You can find various instructional materials on the web or at your local book and video stores. Your local library can be a good source of tapes and recordings. There are television programs and cable networks devoted to such topics as well. Talking with friends, acquaintances, and relatives about their experience with movement practices can also be helpful. You can find practices suitable for lying down, standing, or sitting in various combinations. If you have any medical conditions, be sure to consult your health care provider before choosing your movements. Many professional yoga teachers will be able to help you come up with a set of movements that will be suitable even if you have physical limitations or concerns. It is well worth taking a few classes if you are completely unfamiliar with yoga movements. A teacher can help you tailor and string several movements together for a consistent and safe practice.

Several resources that I use in my classes are Thich Nhat Hanh's (2008) *Mindful Movements,* a DVD from Sounds True; *The Sivananda Companion to Yoga* published by the Sivananda Yoga Center (2000); "The ITP Kata: The Tao of Practice" from the book *The Life We Are Given* by Leonard and Murphy (1995; pp. 73–95); *Mindfulness Yoga: The Awakened Union of Breath, Body, and Mind* by Frank Jude Boccio (2004); and *Yoga for Wellness* by Gary Kraftsow (1999).

I like Thich Nhat Hanh's mindful movements and a set of movements called *sun salutations.* Mindful movements are 10 relatively simple movements that help with stretching and balancing. The whole set can be done in 15 minutes. Sun salutations incorporate several yoga poses into one fluid set of 12 to 14 steps. Doing a few minutes of sun salutations could be an excellent way to stretch and move prior to a sitting meditation. Several variations exist and can be easily accessed through the Internet and viewed on YouTube. *The Sivananda Companion to Yoga* book has very clear pictures that accompany the written descriptions of sun salutations.

Mindfulness of the body is a very rich domain for mindfulness practice. You can be creative, playful, and disciplined all at the same time. I highly recommend some form of body movements and awareness practice prior to a sitting mindfulness practice. I have found a combination of body scan, progressive muscle relaxation, and yoga (e.g., sun salutations and Thich Nhat Hanh's mindful movements) most helpful in preparing for a sitting practice.

I have found that 15 to 30 minutes of movement or yoga and body-related awareness, a few minutes of breathing exercises

(Lessons 13–17), and a 20–30 minute sitting practice are the staples of a strong regular practice.

Many mindfulness practices are exquisitely flexible and versatile and undoubtedly could become a part of your formal or informal practice. Remember, the best practice is the one you do regularly.

CLASS PRACTICE

- *Body scan and progressive muscle relaxation.* Perform a short body scan followed by progressive muscle relaxation and then another short body scan.
- *Mindful standing and movement/yoga.* Stand in stillness for a minute or so before performing 10 to 15 minutes of mindful movements or yoga of your choice.
- *Breath mindfulness.* Perform 15 to 30 minutes of breath mindfulness.
- *Mindful walking.* You can incorporate mindful walking formally or informally in the class as well as outside the class. A few minutes of stretching and mindful walking after your sitting practice is a way to incorporate additional relaxation and body awareness and a short walking practice in the class.
- *Journal.* Describe your experience in detail, especially your experience with yoga/movement. What did you learn? What will you do with this learning? In planning your practice for the week, include any additional sources and resources you need to firm up a set of movements that you may include regularly.
- *End of class.* Perform your chosen ritual to end the class.

LESSON 7

MINDFUL EATING

START THE CLASS

Note: For this class, you will need one raisin to experiment with mindful eating. A raisin is the classic way. However, a grape, a slice of orange, a berry, or another small fruit will work too.

- Perform your start ritual.
- Take a few breaths, inhaling and exhaling fully and slowly.
- Gently close your eyes and come in touch with your intention to learn, experiment with, and practice mindfulness.
- Open your eyes and continue reading.

REVIEW YOUR PRACTICE

How is your practice going? Have you been in contact with your practice buddy? Have you confirmed the yoga/movement set you would like to practice? Have you been practicing mindful breathing, body scan, progressive muscle relaxation, and mindful walking? Are you generally satisfied with your practice? If not, what modifications do you need to make? You may also consider reviewing Lesson 2.

CLASS READING

Mindful Eating

Mindfulness reduces stress partly by inviting us to replace automatic behaviors with awareness and an appreciation for whatever activity we undertake. Mindfulness means one thing at a time. It teaches that even simple, daily activities and chores are worthy of our full attention. Mindfulness protects us from unnecessary multitasking and an automatic-pilot orientation to life. Mindful eating shares the same elements with other mindfulness practices, such as breathing and walking—that is, focused attention, a nonjudgmental attitude, acceptance, staying curious and maintaining a willingness to consider even routine experiences as unique (this is also called the *beginner's mind*), letting go, and relaxing expectations. We can bring mindfulness to all activities, including eating.

In our busy lives, we often forget to really eat and do just that. When was the last time you ate with your focus on what you were eating? When was the last time you really connected with the

eating experience? Each time you eat, is there any conscious recognition that eating, drinking, and breathing are the ways in
which we nurture our body? We tend to eat habitually. We eat
fast. We multitask while we eat. What's more, for many, eating
and food can be a loaded issue. Some struggle with their relationship to food.

There is a body of research that points out links between fast
eating and multitasking during meals and the likelihood of weight
gain and obesity. There are now programs that use mindfulness for
treatment of eating disorders such as binge eating and bulimia.
Research results are promising (Andersen, 2007; Hanh & Cheung,
2010; Kristeller, Baer, & Quillian-Wolver, 2006).

General Instructions on How to Eat Mindfully

Mindful eating can inform what and how much we eat even when
the goal is simply to become more mindful of our daily activities for
general stress reduction. Following are a few practical recommendations to keep in mind for eating mindfully.

- *Just eat.* No multitasking. Make a specific intention to eat
  mindfully for a given meal or a snack. Come to the table to
  eat and do just that—eat. Focus only on the food. Don't
  watch TV, work, or read. Just eat. You can limit conversation or even choose to eat in silence on occasion.
- *Be grateful.* Who prepared the food you are about to eat?
  Who came up with the recipe? Who is the farmer who
  planted the vegetables and cared for them? How did the

food get here? If you really think about it, many people (including yourself) have worked so you could eat this particular food. If you are inclined, acknowledge your gratitude for the food you are about to eat in any way that is meaningful to you.

- *Involve all senses.* Look at everything. Notice the surroundings. Then bring your careful attention to the plate, silverware, and glassware. Look at the food and really see it. Notice the ingredients; notice color, shape, and other visual qualities. Smell the food. Notice various qualities of the smell. Strong or subtle. Can you tell what ingredients are in the food by smelling? Feel the food in your mouth. Notice texture and taste. Can you tell what ingredients are in the food by the taste? Notice the different sounds various foods make as you chew them. Take note of your body's movements while you are eating. What are your habits? Do you tend to bend over toward food? Or do you sit straight and bring the fork or spoon to your mouth? Do you put down your utensils between the bites? Do you use the napkin once or several times throughout the meal? Become aware of your habits, and see what happens when you shift your habitual ways.

- *Notice speed.* Notice how fast or slow you eat. Experiment with the speed of your eating. Try to slow down if you are habitually a fast eater.

- *Notice size.* Notice the bite sizes you take. Experiment with bite sizes. Take bigger and smaller bites than are habitual for you.

- *Chew.* Do you chew once, twice, or more? Try to increase that number severalfold in your next meal. Some teachers recommend to chew 20, 30, or more times before swallowing. What happens to various foods when we chew them more than usual?
- *Notice judgment.* Notice your reaction to food, even subtle reactions. Notice bodily sensations associated with eating. Notice any judgments that arise in response to visual qualities, taste, smell, and texture of the food. Notice emotions that arise. Does a certain color or shape create an impression of what the taste will be? Are previous likes or dislikes coloring your current attitude?
- *Notice swallowing.* Become aware of the desire to swallow. Swallow with awareness, not automatically. If you have chosen a certain number of chews per mouthful, swallow when you reach that number of chews.
- *Have beginner's mind.* Approach each mouthful the same way as if it is the first bite. Stay curious.
- *Refocus.* Acknowledge thoughts, sensations, and emotions when your mind drifts away, and return your attention to the meal.
- *Enjoy.* And above all enjoy what you are eating! Smile as you eat.

Mindfulness of What to Eat

When we pay attention to how we eat and become increasingly aware of our eating, naturally we will also pay more attention to what we eat. What are the ingredients in my food? Where are they coming from? Is the food from a farm, the sea, a distant land, or a nearby community? How and why do I choose what I eat? Am I choosing my food selectively or habitually? What kind of food do I really want to eat? Am I conscious and aware of how the food is affecting me? How is the food affecting my body or even my mind?

The National Center for Complementary and Alternative Medicine provides information on its website (Health Topics A–Z; http://nccam.nih.gov/health/atoz.htm) on a variety of subjects, including herbs, food supplements, and other topics of interest and research related to these topics. Ayurveda, an ancient Eastern system of medicine that considers food as medicine, as well as vegetarian diets have gained much popularity in recent years (Ballentine, 1999; Ladd, 2009; Morningstar & Urmila, 2008).

Instructions for Eating Your Raisin Mindfully

Read the following instructions to eat your raisin mindfully during the practice portion of your class. If you are experimenting with something other than a raisin, adjust the following instructions accordingly:

- Hold the raisin between your fingers.
- Bring your full attention to the raisin.
- Become curious about the raisin as if you have never seen one before. Put yourself in the mind-set of "this is the first time I see this."

- Use all your senses (except taste), including locomotion, to explore and rediscover this raisin.
  - *Look.* Note color, color variations, shape, size, and texture. Hold the raisin up to the light and note any changes.
  - *Smell.* Smell the raisin. Note the strength and type of the smell. Many are surprised to note that there is usually a scent to a raisin.
  - *Touch.* Hold it between your fingers, and feel it in your palm and next to your face. Note the various sensations. Note its degree of softness or hardness.
  - *Listen.* Bring it close to your ears and listen for any sounds as you move it between fingers.
  - *Locomotion.* Note the motions required for your actions.
- Bring the raisin to your mouth. Note any changes that are happening in your mouth in anticipation.
- Put it in your mouth; gently move it around in your mouth. Notice the texture and sensations in the mouth. Notice whether you can taste anything even without biting into it.
- Gently begin the first bite. Note the explosion of taste. Is it one kind of a taste that you are experiencing or more than one?
- Note any emotional response: pleasant, unpleasant, or neutral.
- Chew as many times as you can before swallowing.
- When ready to swallow, note the sensations related to swallowing.

CLASS PRACTICE

- *Body scan and progressive muscle relaxation.* Perform a short body scan, followed by progressive muscle relaxation and then another short body scan.
- *Mindful standing and movement/yoga.* Stand in stillness for a minute or so before performing 10 to 15 minutes of mindful movements or yoga of your choice.
- *Mindful eating.* Eat your raisin according to the previous instructions.
- *Breath mindfulness.* Perform 15 to 30 minutes of breath mindfulness.
- *Mindful walking.* Do a few minutes of stretching and mindful walking.
- *Journal.* Describe your experience in detail, especially your experience of eating the raisin. What did you learn? What will you do with this learning? Journal your thoughts regarding how and what you eat. Incorporating mindful eating into your practice is not a difficult task. Most people find it enjoyable because they begin to really pay attention to and taste their food. Truly tasting the food has helped many to realize how some foods that they have habitually found irresistible do not taste as good as they thought, especially sugary foods. It is best to begin with modest ambitions. Depending on your work and family obligations, it could be more realistic to eat mindfully during the week rather than on the weekends or vice versa. Pick at least one meal during which you can commit to mindful

eating. If eating a whole meal mindfully is unrealistic or intolerable initially, you could commit to eating a few bites mindfully during each meal. Another strategy is to make sure that in each given day you have become mindful of your eating at least once. Remember, mindfulness is about self-care. Consciousness about your eating, the nutrients that enter your body, and the joy and pleasure that can be associated with nurturing yourself are steps in that direction. Some people have successfully included their partner or other family members in practicing mindful eating. This is one of the mindful activities in which you can even enroll children with ease.

- *End of class.* End the class with your ending ritual.

MINDFUL LISTENING TO SOUNDS

START THE CLASS

- Perform your start ritual.
- Take a few breaths, inhaling and exhaling fully and slowly.
- Gently close your eyes and come in touch with your intention to learn, experiment with, and practice mindfulness.
- Open your eyes and continue reading.

REVIEW YOUR PRACTICE

How is your practice going? Have you been in contact with your practice buddy? Have you been more mindful of what and how you eat? Have you been practicing mindfulness of your breath and body? Have you been walking mindfully? Have you been doing yoga or other forms of mindful movements? Are you satisfied with your practice and what you planned? If not, what modifications are needed? You may also consider reviewing Lesson 2.

CLASS READING

Some people find sound to be a more focusing anchor than breath when they sit in meditation practice. As always, my recommendation is to try this practice several times before deciding whether to make it an ongoing practice. Informally, you can incorporate mindfulness of sounds throughout the day for any length of time. Mindfulness of sounds could also be incorporated into the sitting with breath meditation.

- *Pay attention to posture.* Sit upright. Sit tall. Make yourself comfortable. Head balanced. Legs uncrossed if you are sitting on a chair. Shoulders relaxed and away from the ears. Chin slightly tucked in. Chest open. Eyes gently closed.
- *Breathe.* Take a few deep full breaths, inhaling deeply, holding for a moment and then exhaling fully and slowly. Notice the inhalation as the breath goes all the way down into the lungs and the belly, then notice the exhalation as the breath comes back up and out. Breathe in and out through the nose. Trace your "in" breath and "out" breath with awareness.
- *Survey.* Now bring the focus of your attention to the body. Notice sensations that are present in the body, sensations in the feet, legs, thighs, belly, chest, shoulders, neck, and

face. Notice the sensations of the fabric of your clothes on the skin, the sensation of the air on the skin. No need to change anything, just notice. Notice and allow. Turn your attention to thoughts that might be here, right now. Acknowledge the thoughts without getting caught in the stories. Turn your attention to the feeling tone in this moment, the emotional experience. Is it pleasant, unpleasant, or neutral? Notice and then allow what is already here in the body, in the thoughts, and in the mind to be here.

- *Pay attention to sound.* Now let the body sensations, thoughts, emotions, and breath move to the background, turning your full attention to the sounds around you. Give full attention to hearing. Notice soft sounds. Notice loud sounds. Notice silence between the sounds. Notice what is familiar or new, near or far. All sounds are welcome. No need to go after the sounds, no need to strive; let the sounds flow into and out of the field of your awareness.

- *Refocus.* Notice when the mind wanders, and gently bring the focus of your attention back to sounds. There is no right or wrong way to do this. Notice any thoughts, judgments, or emotions with friendliness, and then bring the attention back to sounds.

- *End the practice.* Gently open your eyes when the practice ends.

In the mindfulness class that I teach, a participant shared her experiences concerning the effectiveness of sound mindfulness. She told us that in the past, each time she went to the hairdresser, she became irritated and impatient with the noisy environment. She could not wait to get out. She always delayed her haircuts and getting her nails done because of the noise. This time, however, she listened to the sounds mindfully. To her amazement, when she let go of her previous impressions and opened herself to discovery, she found a rich array of sounds. The soft and loud humming sounds of several hairdryers, background music, and conversations all blended splendidly, as if she were listening to a symphony.

CLASS PRACTICE

- *Body scan and progressive muscle relaxation.* Perform a short body scan followed by progressive muscle relaxation and then another short body scan.
- *Mindful standing and movement/yoga.* Stand in stillness for a minute or so before performing 10 to 15 minutes of mindful movements or yoga of your choice.
- *Breath mindfulness.* Perform 15 minutes of breath mindfulness.
- *Mindfulness of the sounds.* Continue with mindfulness of the sounds as described previously for 15 minutes.
- *Mindful walking.* Do a few minutes of stretching and mindful walking.
- *Journal.* Describe your experience of sound mindfulness in detail. What did you notice? Is there a difference between the way you habitually listen and this way of listening? Are you noticing anything else? What will you do with this learning? Incorporate mindful listening to sounds formally and informally.
- *End of class.* Perform your chosen ritual to end the class.

LESSON 9

MINDFUL SILENCE

START THE CLASS

- Perform your start ritual.
- Take a few breaths, inhaling and exhaling fully and slowly.
- Gently close your eyes and come in touch with your intention to learn, experiment with, and practice mindfulness.
- Open your eyes and continue reading.

REVIEW YOUR PRACTICE

How is your practice going? Have you been in contact with your practice buddy? Have you been more mindful of what and how you eat? Have you been mindful of the sounds around you, and have you incorporated this into your mindfulness of the breath? Have you been walking mindfully? How about yoga or mindful movements? Are you generally satisfied with your practice? If no, what could be modified? You may also consider reviewing Chapter 2.

CLASS READING

Silence can produce a sense of calm and peace. It can deepen attention to all experience and facilitate contemplation. It can enhance and heighten the awareness of various sensory input.

To enhance relaxation and inner focus, many meditation retreats and programs include silence as a practice. In addition to forgoing conversation, silence can include refraining from activities such as reading, writing, or engaging in other modes of communication. This form of silence is referred to as *noble silence,* a practice that dates back several thousand years. Noble silence is practiced in Hinduism, Buddhism, and other monastic traditions. Gandhi observed silence every Monday for most of his life. An extreme example is Mehr Baba, an Indian mystic and spiritual master who maintained silence for several decades. Monastic trainings can include silence for very long periods, that is, months or years. Silence and chanting are incorporated into the training of monks in monasteries in part to enhance the ability to listen. There is literature that supports the virtues of silence and the hazards of noise (Bernardi, Porta, & Sleight, 2006; Dossey, 2008; Feiss, 1999; Jina, 2003; Paul, 2004; Voisin, Bidet-Caulet, Bertrand, & Fonlupt, 2006; Willich, Wegscheider, Stallmann, & Keil, 2006).

We become so habituated to the noises in our environment that we no longer even hear them. During a recent vacation, I became acutely aware of silence, with awe and amusement. I had travelled to a remote mountainous area. The silence was so deep and profound there that I believe the complete absence of noise woke me up in the middle of the night. I had not experienced such a level of silence in a long time, and I had grown unaccustomed to it.

In a typical 1-week mindfulness-based stress reduction training in a retreat setting, about 2 days are spent in silence. In 8-week mindfulness trainings, usually around Week 6 of the training, 6 to 8 hours are spent in silence. There are advanced trainings that are held in complete silence for several days to several months or more. Khalil Gibran (1988), poet and writer, in his renowned book, *The Prophet,* has a beautiful piece on silence. He wrote, "You talk when you cease to be at ease with your thoughts; and when you no longer dwell in the solitude of your heart you live in your lips, and sound is a diversion and a pastime" (pp. 60–61).

If you live alone, you may think that you already are silent a lot. Mindful silence, however, is more than simply not talking. It is an active silence. During the silence, you are attending to and actively sensing with all your senses. A serene setting does enhance the experience, but it is not necessary to be in a perfect environment. You may try to chop vegetables, cook, eat, or fold the clothes in mindful silence and attention. No radio, TV, phone conversation, or reading printed materials. Stay observant and mindful of thoughts, which you may find become more active during periods of silence. Redirect your attention to your sensory experiences.

Mindfulness classes often include silence as part of a "mindful day of retreat" (usually from 9 a.m. to 3 or 4 p.m.). In one of the retreats I offered in 2010, one participant expressed a great deal of gratitude for the day spent in silence. This was a completely new experience for him. He had been concerned the night before that this day would be intolerable and boring. To his surprise, the time had flown by much faster than he had imagined it would. He initially felt uncomfortable and "rude" because he was not greeting other participants with either words or expressions. But after an hour or so he warmed up to the experience and felt relieved and "free." He felt he was given "permission" to not observe social niceties and obligations. He no longer felt obliged to attend to anything but his own experiences. He felt his attention to mindful breathing, walking, observing, and moving increased during silence. In particular, during the lunch hour, he pleasantly discovered the meaning of "true" mindful eating by taking his time to savor the food and allow different tastes and textures to "bathe" his sight, taste, and smell. He also felt that the silence made it easier to do things slowly. The slowing down contributed to his ability to observe and attend to the details of his experiences. At the conclusion of the day he said, "I feel so peaceful I wanted the silence to go on much longer."

CLASS PRACTICE

- *Attend to silence.* Become aware of silence during this class.
- *Body scan and progressive muscle relaxation.* Perform a short body scan followed by progressive muscle relaxation and then another short body scan.
- *Mindful standing and movement/yoga.* Stand in stillness for a minute or so before performing 10 to 15 minutes of mindful movements or yoga of your choice.

- *Breath mindfulness.* Perform 15 to 30 minutes of breath mindfulness. Incorporate mindfulness of sounds.
- *Mindful walking.* Do a few minutes of stretching and mindful walking.
- *Journal.* What did you notice about silence during the class? Describe your experience. What will you do with this learning? Consider incorporating a period of silence into your weekly practice. Experiment with different lengths of silence if you can. You may think it is not possible to be silent among other household members. You would need to prepare and inform them ahead of time. In some retreats, when there is more than one workshop during the same period, those participants who are observing silence wear a sign that reads "In Silence," designating their silent status. This signals the community not to engage them in conversation. You can be creative and devise a way of letting your household members know if you wish to practice silence. After a couple of giggles and eyes rolling, most people quickly get used to the idea. You will also find that you may even create curiosity and interest in others to practice silence. One particular time that silence can be integrated playfully in family life is during mealtimes.
- *End of class.* Perform your chosen ritual to end the class.

MINDFUL SEEING

START THE CLASS

Note: During this lesson you will need a leaf to experiment with mindful seeing. A seashell, a flower, a small stone, or another small nature item will work too.

- Perform your start ritual.
- Take a few breaths, inhaling and exhaling fully and slowly.
- Gently close your eyes and come in touch with your intention to learn, experiment with, and practice mindfulness.
- Open your eyes and continue reading.

REVIEW YOUR PRACTICE

How is your practice going? Have you been in contact with your practice buddy? Did you incorporate a period of silence into your practice last week? Have you been more mindful of what and how you eat? Have you been mindful of the sounds around you, and have you incorporated this awareness into your mindfulness of the breath? Have you been walking mindfully? How about yoga or mindful movements? Are you generally satisfied with your practice? If not, what needs to be modified? You may also consider reviewing Chapter 2.

CLASS READING

Contemplation is a powerful way of practicing, discovering, and deepening one's understanding of the universe. Some practitioners have solely relied on contemplation to deepen their spiritual lives. The brevity of this section belies the power of this mode of meditation and practice. The quality of mindful attention to seeing (i.e., contemplation) does not depend on the subject itself (e.g., the leaf); rather, it depends on the quality of attention we give it. James Green (1994), an experienced meditator and teacher, described *contemplation* as actively looking at something without using words. He said that the task is to have a direct experience with whatever we choose to look at. The eye sees and the mind sees without any intervening step. This is not easy to do because our minds are usually busy converting the images we see into words as if we were describing them to someone else. Descriptive words are indeed wonderful tools to use on those occasions when we need to convey a scene to others. But most of the time we do not. Rarely do words capture the richness and the subtleties of our true experiences. Contemplation teaches us to see without the filter of descriptive or judgmental words. When we do not use word filters, we gain a direct and instant knowing. By seeing this way, our view is enormously enlarged. When we learn to see with our whole attention, the world that emerges in our view is filled with infinite wonder and uniqueness.

In the mindfulness class that I teach, one participant described his experience of mindful seeing during a special cruise vacation he took with his wife of 30 years. He said cruising the Alaskan and Canadian shores was an exhilarating experience. The practice of "seeing" mindfully enhanced the natural beauty of the northern coastline. He said, "Close your eyes and imagine hundreds of miles of snow-covered mountains, blue ice, the rare sighting of wildlife, and the birth of a sliver of ice from the frozen coastline." For him, the hours spent really being aware of these wonders were a blessing. He added that before leaving this planet, one should "consider giving this gift to yourself."

For the mindful seeing experiment, you will need a leaf. If you are experimenting with something other than a leaf, adjust the instructions accordingly. Approach this experiment with a kind, friendly, curious, and gentle manner. Consider the leaf the subject of your exploration, not an object to be used. Manifest the sense of wonder, respect, and awe you feel when visiting a beautiful place in nature. Set aside 10 to 15 minutes for this experiment.

- Look at the leaf with the full focus of your attention.
- Let go of words as you explore the leaf. Sometimes it helps to know you will not be reporting what you see to another person. You want a direct connection with the leaf without the mediation of words. Words and verbal mediation are

deeply rooted in our minds, but with practice the direct connection is possible. For example, there are no words to describe all the shades of green or other colors you will discover.

- Look at every detail. Notice all the shades of color.
- Hold the leaf up to the light and look at it, then experiment with different levels of light and note the shifts in what you see.
- Look at it from various distances—for example, close up or at arm's length.
- Look at the back of the leaf with the same attention.
- Include touch and smell in the experience.
- Where is the mind wandering to? Gently bring it back.
- Get to know your leaf so well that you could find it among a hundred leaves if you needed to.
- Bring your experiment to an end.

CLASS PRACTICE

- *Body scan and progressive muscle relaxation.* Perform a short body scan followed by progressive muscle relaxation and then another short body scan.
- *Mindful standing and movement/yoga.* Stand in stillness for a minute or so before performing 10 to 15 minutes of mindful movements or yoga of your choice.
- *Breath and sound mindfulness.* Perform 20 to 30 minutes of breath mindfulness. Incorporate mindfulness of sounds in the first few minutes. Stay mindful of silence during the

class. Mindful attention to sounds enhances the experience of stillness between the sounds.

- *Mindful seeing.* Continue with contemplating the leaf or another object for 10 minutes.
- *Mindful walking.* Do a few minutes of stretching and mindful walking.
- *Journal.* What did you notice? Is there a difference between the way you habitually look at things and this way of looking? Describe your experience in detail. What will you do with this learning? Look at as many objects as possible with a mindful eye. You may want to make a point of seeing one or two subjects mindfully each day. In particular, natural items such as shells, stones, flowers, trees, stars, and the night sky, when contemplated for a time, can result in profound experiences and feelings of connectedness to nature, the universe, and beyond.
- *End of class.* Perform your chosen ritual to end the class.

MINDFUL INTERACTIONS

START THE CLASS

- Perform your start ritual.
- Take a few breaths, inhaling and exhaling fully and slowly.
- Gently close your eyes and come in touch with your intention to learn, experiment with, and practice mindfulness.
- Open your eyes and continue reading.

REVIEW YOUR PRACTICE

How is your practice going? Have you been in contact with your practice buddy? What object(s) did you contemplate last week? Did you incorporate a period of silence into your practice? Have you been more mindful of what and how you eat? Have you been mindful of the sounds around you, and have you incorporated this awareness into your mindfulness of the breath? Have you been walking mindfully? Contemplation and mindful walking can be integrated for rewarding results. How about yoga or mindful movements? Are you generally satisfied with your practice? If not, what needs to be modified?

You have come a long way from the beginning of this book. If you have practiced mindfulness with some regularity, both formally and informally, you might have noted some shifts or changes in your habitual ways. You might have come to realize how regular practice affects your mind and body, albeit in subtle ways. Do not underestimate the importance of subtle shifts and changes. The following note from a class participant is an example of such shifts:

I have been noticing what is around me more. I had never paid attention to the beautiful painting that is hanging in the entrance to my building before. Actually I had neglected to really see any of them. Noticing the small pleasant things has been a lot of fun. The other day at work I slowly walked by some flowers when I was going from one building to another. There were several bushes of yellow, red, white, and pink roses lining the wall of the pedestrian sidewalk. I smelled several roses and reflected on the fragrance, one from each bush. Some had a very distinct fragrance and some had a mild fragrance and some had no obvious fragrance. An amused security officer passed by and said, "You are really smelling the roses." I told him which one had the most distinct fragrance. He proceeded to smell a couple of bushes and find out for himself. We both laughed lightheartedly and wished each other a good day and departed. It all lasted 1 or 1.5 minutes. The smell of the roses and the communication that followed with the officer both were quite pleasant. I kept reflecting back on this experience for the rest of the day with a sense of pleasure.

CLASS READING

Verbal communications are enhanced with mindful listening and seeing. Mindful interaction with another person means staying present, nonjudgmental, open, and curious. It means accepting another person as he or she is, letting go of previous impressions, and letting go of any goals or expectations you may have for the interaction.

- Look at and truly see the person you are interacting with. Attend to the person. Notice what the person is wearing, the colors, the size and shape of the person's body, his or her facial expressions, the color of the person's eyes and hair—not to form judgments, but rather to really see the person. Do you remember the eye color of the last stranger you talked to?
- Listen to what is said. Keep a mindful approach to conversations. It is easier to apply mindful attention to a neutral content. However, when the content includes sentiments that either demonstrate the feelings of the speaker or simulate feelings in the listener or both, the task of mindful communications requires more attention. Going back in time to judge or going forward in time to formulate your opinion or response detracts from mindful listening. Listen without preconception and expectation. Thinking about your answer is a form of multitasking. When you are listening, only listen. Listen to the words, to the tone, to the pitch, and to the content.
- Respond thoughtfully. Pay attention to your choice of words. Do you have a sense of what nonverbal messages

you are providing? Notice your own thoughts and emotions, and keep the witness, the observer, the "I" active in the process. Take note of your own reactivity, either positive or negative. In time, you will develop an awareness of what you bring to a variety of interactions.

- Notice when your mind wanders, and bring it back to the present time and place.

- Maintain a gentle, kind, nonjudgmental, and accepting attitude during the interaction to the extent possible. Notice when your mind becomes judgmental and attempt to resume a nonjudgmental stance, either toward yourself or toward others.

- Bring in an attitude of curiosity, a genuine desire to know more about this person. If you notice something that catches your attention about what this person is telling you, inquire further. Say, "Tell me more about___."

- Be the listener/the communicator that you would like in a partner. See and hear in the ways in which you would like to be seen and heard.

In my mindfulness class, one participant noted the impact of mindfulness in her interactions with her friends:

> I have a group of friends from high school and about every six months we have a "girls' weekend" at the beach, where one of our friends lives. It's true that the older we get, the more judgmental we can sometimes become. When you're around a group of women that you've known for over 40 years, you also tend to be very competitive. I've noticed that during the last two outings I have tried to move away from being so judgmental and

opinionated and much more open to accepting these women as they are and realizing that we all have flaws. I love them all dearly, but women sometimes can just be women. I firmly believe that my practice of mindfulness around self-acceptance, judgment, and mindfulness in communications has really helped me forge an even stronger relationship with these women and so for that, I am eternally grateful.

Another class participant said,

I have tried asking, "Tell me more." when I was curious with those I have interacted with people during the week. It has resulted in a more genuine and warm conversation with my colleagues. In one conversation I was even able to share the feelings of rejection I have had about nobody remembering my birthday this year when everyone else's was acknowledged in our weekly staff meetings. One colleague shared that hers was forgotten too and I was not the only one. We ended up laughing about how childish and yet normal it was to feel neglected.

CLASS PRACTICE

- *Body scan and progressive muscle relaxation.* Perform a short body scan, followed by progressive muscle relaxation and then another short body scan.
- *Mindful standing and movement/yoga.* Stand in stillness for a minute or so before performing 10 to 15 minutes of mindful movements or yoga of your choice.
- *Breath and sound mindfulness.* Perform 20 to 30 minutes of breath mindfulness. Incorporate mindfulness of sounds in the first few minutes. Stay aware of your experience of silence during the class.

- *Mindful seeing.* Contemplate something in your surroundings for a few minutes.
- *Mindful walking.* Do a few minutes of stretching and mindful walking.
- *Journal.* What have you learned? What will you do with this learning? During the week, look for opportunities to engage in communications mindfully. Experiment with loved ones, in work situations, or with strangers. Look, listen, hear, accept, and stay curious and present. Let go of expectations. When you hear something that catches your attention, say, "Tell me more." Note the quality of your interaction. Be sure to journal about such interactions afterward.
- *End of class.* Perform your chosen ritual to end the class.

LESSON 12

MINDFUL CONSUMPTION

START THE CLASS

- Perform your start ritual.
- Take a few breaths, inhaling and exhaling fully and slowly.
- Gently close your eyes and come in touch with your intention to learn, experiment with, and practice mindfulness.
- Open your eyes and continue reading.

REVIEW YOUR PRACTICE

How is your practice going? Have you been in contact with your practice buddy? Have you been aware of interacting mindfully with loved ones or others? Have you been saying "tell me more" when appropriate, showing your interest and curiosity in your loved ones or others? What object did you contemplate last week? Did you incorporate a period of silence into your practice? Have you been more mindful of what and how you eat? Have you been mindful of the sounds around you and have you incorporated this into your mindfulness of the breath? Have you been walking mindfully? Contemplation and mindful walking can be integrated for rewarding results. How about yoga or mindful movements? Are you generally satisfied with your practice? If not, what do you need to modify? Or you can persist one more week and observe any shifts or changes.

CLASS READING

To better understand and become mindful consumers, we need to understand the difference between two related concepts, hunger and appetite. *Hunger* is a natural need for food, whereas *appetite* is a learned and conditioned craving. Appetite is an acquired habit and has little to do with hunger. The same concept can be applied to thirst and other needs. We can become increasingly more mindful of our thirst/hunger to satisfy a real need versus the variety of false appetites we have acquired over time during our life history (Ramacharaka, 1931). With mindful attention, we can distinguish between our needs and the cravings that rule us by the force of habit. How sweet life would be if we delighted in a piece of bread, a bite from an apple, a cool gulp of fresh water, and the simplest expressions of love and caring in conversation. Conquering habits of consumption is a tall order. Mindfulness gives us the tools to step in that direction; it gives us the tools to try, not by fighting ourselves but by allowing, accepting, and understanding what is happening inside of us to begin the examination of our true needs versus our habitual appetites.

Buddhist teacher Thich Nhat Hanh (1992a) has discussed the importance of the sources that nourish our mind and body. He has indicated that anything that enters our body—food, what we hear or listen to, what we watch and see, or other sensory information and stimulation—deeply influences us. Everything we ingest in its larger sense can be a source of nutrition that impacts our mind, body, and spirit. What we eat, listen to, smell, watch, see, read, or touch are all sources of input. We need to be mindful of and attentive to what we allow inside our body. Are we choosing our food, music, TV programs, and readings mindfully? Or are we passive consumers? How many negative influences are we allowing in? Are we allowing toxins through what we eat? What we see or read? What we listen to? We may not have choices for all items of consumption. But if we pay attention, we become aware of toxins that we allow in our bodies because of habit or negligence. The body is the "temple." With mindfulness, we can take better care of ourselves.

Now reflect on all sources of sensory input to your body in the following domains:

- *Food.* What foods am I eating? Which ones are consistent with my beliefs about food and nutrition and caring for my body? What do I need to eat more of? What do I need to eat less of? Why? Do I want to make modifications to how and what I eat?
- *Sounds.* What do I hear? What do I listen to? Am I choosing? Do I like music? Do I like music all the time? What

kind do I like? Do I like periods of silence? When would silence be preferable to having a source of sound around? What do I want to listen to or hear more of? What do I want to listen to or hear less of? How does my body feel when I listen to sounds that I like? How does it feel when I hear things that I do not like? Can I be more selective in accordance with caring for my body?

- *Sights.* What do I look at? What do I read? What do I watch? Am I selecting and selective? What kind of things would I like to see more of? What kinds of things do I want to see less of? How does my body feel when I see violent or thrilling scenes? How does my body feel when I see nature? Am I maintaining a balance among things I want to see?

- *Smell.* What kind of scents do I have around me? Am I choosing them? What do I want more of? What do I want less of? Why? Do I need to make modifications and choices?

- *Touch.* What kinds of experiences do I have? Am I touching people with my words? With my hands? Am I aware of what I touch during the day? Do I hug and touch my children or loved ones? Do I receive enough touch myself? Who can I ask for what I need?

- *Interactions/social activities.* Who do I interact with during the day? Am I making choices? Who would I like to interact with more? Who would I like to interact with less? How am I interacting with them? Am I mindful of the modes of interaction?

The main idea is to become more conscious of habitual consumption patterns as we exercise mindfulness. Instead of reactivity, we can exercise choice. We are facing choices more often than we think. We may not want to see it that way. Inquiry into our choices often invites mindful inquiry into attachment and its two sides: avoidance and craving. The mindful exploration of avoidance and craving can provide valuable and even surprising revelations. Notice whether there are areas of consumption in your life you would like to become more mindful of.

A participant in my mindfulness class examined her attachments and noted that she had become increasingly aware of the various decorative objects in her home. She noticed that each individual object was clean and beautiful. Yet her house felt cluttered, and dusting was a huge chore. She chose not to go to the stores where she would be tempted to buy more of these objects for a while. Although it was difficult at first, she then began giving away a selection of her household decorations to loved ones for various occasions instead of buying new gifts. Her goal was to let go of her "beautiful clutter." She began with objects that she could give away with ease. Over time, she was able to let go of many objects that were not easy to part with, including a beloved but not functioning antique grandfather clock. She selected each gift with care and paid attention to her own thoughts and feelings. She stated that she did not miss any of these objects and very much appreciated the simplified decoration and increased spaciousness of her home. She has also become very selective and mindful of her new purchases, asking herself, "Do I need this or do I simply want it?" She was aware that she did not want to reclutter her home with more beautiful objects.

Another class participant decided to pay more attention to his consumption of sounds. He noted that when he woke up in the morning, he habitually turned the TV on, made coffee, and began his day. He noted that he was not listening to the programs. It was simply a background noise. He wondered if he disliked silence. He decided to experiment with this and did not turn the TV on. Quickly he felt much more peaceful and realized that he actually liked the silence of his home in the morning. Mornings became the favorite time for his journaling. From time to time he chose a select piece of music to listen to.

CLASS PRACTICE

- *Body scan and progressive muscle relaxation.* Perform a short body scan, followed by progressive muscle relaxation and then another short body scan.
- *Mindful standing and movement/yoga.* Stand in stillness for a minute or so before performing 10 to 15 minutes of mindful movements or yoga of your choice.
- *Breath and sound mindfulness.* Perform 20 to 30 minutes of breath mindfulness. Incorporate mindfulness of sounds in the first few minutes. Stay aware of your experience of silence in the class.
- *Mindful seeing.* Contemplate something in your surroundings for a few minutes.
- *Mindful walking.* Do a few minutes of stretching and mindful walking.
- *Journal.* What is your reaction to the reading and reflecting on your consumption habits? What have you learned?

What will you do with this learning? This lesson introduces a number of important concepts and possibilities for practice. You may find that you would like to spend some time on this topic to address and shape your choices in various domains with increased awareness and consciousness. If you are interested in becoming a more mindful consumer, you may want to arrange the domains that you wish to change or modify in their order of difficulty. Choose an area of most comfort and least struggle. Observe your behavior in that category mindfully for a week, and journal daily. Decide what you would like to do more of and what you would like to do less of in that domain. Arrange your practice plan accordingly, and keep track. When you feel sufficiently comfortable with one area of sensory practice, then you may choose to move to the next area. It is best to engage the hardest area last. There's no rush. If you need to stay on a given domain for several weeks to feel solid about your practice, do so before moving to another domain or level of difficulty.

- *End of class.* Perform your chosen ritual to end the class.

LESSON 13

ABDOMINAL BREATHING

START THE CLASS

- Perform your start ritual.
- Take a few breaths, inhaling and exhaling fully and slowly.
- Gently close your eyes, and come in touch with your intention to learn, experiment with, and practice mindfulness.
- Open your eyes and continue reading.

REVIEW YOUR PRACTICE

How is your practice going? Have you been in contact with your practice buddy? Have you chosen an area of consumption to address and become mindful of? Have you been aware of interacting mindfully with loved ones or others? Have you been saying "tell me more" when appropriate, showing your interest and curiosity in your loved ones or others? What object did you contemplate last week? Did you incorporate a period of silence into your practice? Have you been more mindful of what and how you eat? Have you been mindful of the sounds around you, and have you possibly incorporated this awareness into your mindfulness of the breath? Have you been walking mindfully? Contemplation and mindful walking can be integrated for rewarding results. How about yoga or mindful movements? Are you generally satisfied with your practice? If not, what needs to be modified? Or do you believe you need to persist a bit longer before deciding to make changes?

CLASS READING

Life is but a series of breaths.

—Yogi Ramacharaka

Controlling the breath is a prerequisite to controlling the mind and the body.

—Swami Rama

Mindfulness is about becoming conscious of our experience, moment to moment. Breath can be a very powerful tool on the road to developing consciousness. Do you remember Thich Nhat Hanh's definition of mindfulness? He said *mindfulness* is to know when you are breathing in and to know when you are breathing out. The more you keep yourself aware of your breath, the more mindful you become. Mindfulness of our natural breathing in and of itself is an effective and complete mindfulness practice. Mindful breathing is described in full detail in Lesson 1, but here we revisit the main feature of this practice, which is to simply observe the flow of breath without attempting to exert control. Simple awareness of the breath can promote deeper, more regular, and calmer breathing, which has a relaxing effect on the body and a quieting effect on the mind. Just becoming aware of the breathing process engages the cerebral cortex and stimulates the more evolved areas of the brain, our consciousness.

Lessons 13 through 17 provide information about breathing practices other than mindful breathing that are also known to promote awareness, consciousness, and health (Block, Arnott, Quigley, & Lynch, 1989; Bodhananda, 1995; Brown & Gerberg 2005a, 2005b; Evans et al., 2009; Higashi, 1964; Klein, Pilon, Prosser, & Shannahoff-Khalsa, 1986; Rama, Ballentine, & Haynes, 2007; Ramacharaka, 1905; Saraswati, 2002; Shannahoff-Khalsa, 2007; Shannahoff-Khalsa, Boyle, & Buebel, 1991; Telles, Raghuraj, Maharana, & Nagendra, 2007; Weil, 2000). Class readings for these lessons will be limited to specific breathing techniques. The techniques can be calming or relaxing, energizing, balancing, or some combination of these states. Many breathing techniques tend to increase lung ventilation and flow of oxygen in the body and help to connect us to the finer details of the mental processes as well. Mindful breathing, abdominal breathing, full breath (yogic breath or three-part breath), rhythmic breath, alternate nostril breathing, and *kapalbhati* (energetic breathing) are among the most popular breathing exercises. For each of these techniques, the exercise is introduced and then, if possible, the rationale behind its popularity is explained.

Breathing exercises are powerful. They can be practiced formally or informally. Informally, you can take a few mindful or other types of breath anytime, anywhere. Formally, you can set aside a specific time to practice them. These are versatile practices and can be practiced sitting, standing, or lying down. Try to practice each type of breathing just by itself a few times until you begin to appreciate its unique effects. Various breath exercises can be incorporated into a practice that combines several components. For example, in your daily practice, you can begin with a body scan or progressive muscle relaxation, followed by alternate nostril breathing (see Lesson 16), followed by mindfulness of the breath in a sitting meditation. You can choose how long you would like to devote to each. You can do 10-10-10 minutes for a total practice time of 30 minutes or 15-15-15 minutes for a total of 45 minutes. It can be 5-10-15 minutes or any other combination. The key is that after choosing your desired combination, keep practicing it regularly. Pay attention to the class practice combinations offered with each lesson to get ideas about organizing your daily practice combinations.

Breath is life. Our habitual breathing patterns matter. What we breathe and how we breathe have an impact on our physical body, emotional body, and energy body. The more attention we pay to our breathing, the more conscious we become of subtle and obvious effects of breathing on various layers of our being. The nervous system, respiratory system, heart and circulation system, and hormonal system are all particularly sensitive to the impact of breathing and flow of oxygen in the body.

Catch yourself at various times of the day, during various activities and emotional states. Take note of your breathing. Is it continuous, full, and smooth? Or is it irregular, fast, shallow, or noisy? If you find any of the latter, choose one of the breathing exercises that fit best. Apply it by bringing conscious control and attention to the breath. You will begin to regulate processes that you may have thought were beyond your influence. Remember, you are breathing anyway and anywhere. Bringing consciousness to it is a choice that is available to you at all times, whether you are sitting, standing, or lying down or whether you are at home, outdoors, at work, on the street, or driving. Even in states of physical illness, conscious awareness of the breath is possible. Breath practice is simple and accessible and yields generous rewards.

Breath and its implications have interested the ancient yogis and modern scientist alike. Some yogis have spent decades or even their entire lives studying the breath and its effects on the body, energy, mind, and spiritual development. In the East, entire schools have been dedicated to understanding, studying, and working on the complicated relationship among these variables. There is a substantial literature on the art and science of conscious breath, or *pranayama*.

Energy and breath are intimately connected. With each breath, energy flows through the body. The body energy is a complex system and network of flowing currents, with constant reciprocity between the energy inside and the energy outside of the body in the form of nutrition, air, water, and light. All aspects of breathing—rhythm, pattern, quality, and quantity—provide information and signal what is happening inside the body.

The breathing system can come under both voluntary (conscious) and involuntary (unconscious) control. Unconscious control of the breath originates in the brain stem, a more primitive part of the brain. Conscious control of the breath comes from the cerebral cortex, the more evolved part of the brain. The cerebral cortex can keep the breath under voluntary control.

Breath and emotions are closely connected. The rate, intensity, and depth of breathing can change during fear, anxiety, deep thinking, excitement, sadness, and other emotions. A calm, slow, and rhythmic breath usually indicates a relaxed state. Irregular, shallow, rapid, or noisy breathing can indicate tension, stress, or excitement. During anxiety states and fear, the breath tends to become shallow and rapid. When one is angry, the breath can be short and forceful. When sad, it may be arrhythmic or gasping, or there can be sighing. The idea is this: If the emotional states influence the breath, then the breath can be consciously monitored to impact the emotional states. This of course does not happen overnight, and it takes practice to bring the unconscious and automatic process of breathing under voluntary control. Mindfulness of the breath can give us a thermostat, a window, into our experience in each moment (Bodhananda, 1995; Rama, Ballentine, & Haynes, 2007; Ramacharaka, 1905).

The same idea is behind biofeedback, which has been successfully used in the management of blood pressure, migraine, and even seizure activity and other health issues. The Association for Applied Psychophysiology and Biofeedback defined *biofeedback* as the process of gaining greater awareness of many physiological functions primarily by using instruments that provide precise information on the activity of brain waves, heart function, breathing, muscle activity, and skin temperature. These instruments rapidly feed back information to the user until the user learns to control and to change these physiological activities at will. Over time, these changes can endure without continued use of an instrument (Schwartz & Olson, 2003).

General Considerations for Breathing Exercises

An infinite number of breathing techniques have been perfected by the yogis to promote health and well-being and proper care of the body. The breath control techniques promote and influence mind–body interaction and the flow of life force or energy (known as *prana*) in the body. One does not have to embrace the full yogic philosophy of life to appreciate the many health benefits of their knowledge and practices. This rich tradition of caring for the body as the "temple" of the spirit offers sensitively rendered guidance on methods of nutrition, water/fluid consumption, breathing, exercise, cleanliness, and rest.

In recent years, Western researchers have become increasingly interested in better understanding the mechanisms and healing powers of breathing techniques. The field is exquisitely complex given the number and variations of the breathing techniques and their impact on various body systems including the nervous system. Richard Brown and his colleagues at Columbia University (Brown & Gerberg, 2005a, 2005b) have studied several breathing techniques and their impact on the nervous system functions. They reported that breathing techniques are a powerful tool that can adjust imbalances of the autonomic nervous system and influence a broad range of physical and emotional functions. Various studies have shown the effects of the breath on cardiac vagal tone and autonomic nervous system functions. These effects are achieved by decreasing sympathetic and increasing parasympathetic activity (see Chapter 1 for a discussion of sympathetic and parasympathetic responses) and by influencing the neuroendocrine functioning, such as cortisol and possibly vasopressin and oxytocin levels (Brown & Gerberg, 2005a, 2005b; Higashi, 1964).

Caution

Breathing techniques are powerful. They affect the nervous system, blood circulation, oxygenation, heart, and the endocrine system. Do not overdo any of them. Always start with a few or short periods and assess how you feel before increasing your practice efforts. Some lightheadedness, dizziness, or tingling can occur during breathing exercises. Consult with your health care professional if you have questions or concerns. Anyone with respiratory disorders, cardiovascular disease, high blood pressure, pregnancy, seizure disorders, serious mental illness, or other serious health issues should consult a health care provider before engaging in complex or prolonged breathing practices.

Proper body posture is important to obtain the full benefits from the breathing exercises in Lessons 13 through 17. Straight back and neck alignment in the spine, open chest, relaxed shoulders, and slightly tucked-in chin (to align neck and spine) is the recommended posture. One rule of thumb is to never strain anything. Stretch yes, strain no. Many breathing techniques can be done in any position—lying down, sitting, or standing.

All the exercises in Lessons 13 through 17 presume nose breathing unless specifically indicated. The intention is for breath to flow through the nostrils and not the open mouth. It is recommended that all the exercises be done on an empty stomach and not after eating. Keep yourself hydrated at all times.

Abdominal Breathing

Abdominal breathing is also known as *belly* or *diaphragmatic breathing.* It is a commonly recommended form of breathing that engages the lower part of the lungs that are seldom used in our habitual manner of breathing. Babies are belly breathers. As we grow older, we become more and more chest or neck breathers, using the upper parts of the lungs. It is important to engage the lower parts of the lungs. Done properly, abdominal breathing uses the full lung capacity, provides a massaging function to lungs and internal organs, and is considered a health-promoting approach to breathing.

In this form of breathing, you ideally will notice the rise and fall of your belly in the inhalation and exhalation, respectively. If you do not know how to breathe abdominally, it might be easier to learn it while lying down. It could also be practiced in sitting or standing positions.

- *Lie down.* Get in a comfortable position on your back.
- *Breathe.* Bring your attention inward and take a few mindful breaths.
- *Take inventory of body sensations, thoughts, and feelings.* Take a head-to-toe inventory of the body. Notice the sensations in the body. Notice any thoughts that are present.

Notice the emotional tone of the moment. Acknowledge all that is present. Let go of the sensations, thoughts, emotions—allow them to go to the background—and gently bring your attention to the breath. Bring curiosity and the beginner's mind to this experience.

- *Establish your intention.* Decide how long you would like to breathe abdominally. It is recommended to start with a few minutes or 10 to 12 breaths. Adjust the duration as needed.
- *Feel your abdomen as you breathe.* Place one or both hands on the region that seems to rise and fall the most as you inhale and exhale. Become aware of the area you are naturally using most in your breathing. Now put one or both hands on the lower abdomen below your naval; breathe into this area. Notice how your hand(s) rise and fall as you inhale and exhale in a conscious manner. If it is still difficult to breathe in and out of the abdomen, gently press your hand down as you exhale fully, letting the abdomen push your hand back up as you inhale. The pressure of your hand increases awareness of the movement of your belly during abdominal breathing.
- *Breathe deeply.* Breathe in deeply and fully down into your lungs, filling up the lower part of the lungs with air. The belly will expand in the inhalation. At the exhalation the belly goes back toward the spine. Notice when you are breathing in. Notice when you are breathing out. Notice the flow of air moving through the nostrils and down into the lungs in the inhalation, belly expanding, holding, letting go, exhal-

ing, the air coming out of the nostrils in the exhalation, and the belly going back toward the spine. Follow and trace the breath as it goes in and comes out. You may put your hand on the lower part of the belly and feel the expansion and contraction of the belly.

- *Refocus.* Notice when the mind wanders to thoughts, emotions, sensations, or sounds. Notice these natural states with kindness and gentleness, and bring the attention back to the breath each time. Remind yourself of the attitude of acceptance toward whatever arises in the mind. Gently return the attention back to the breath. Remember, there is no right or wrong way to do this.
- *End.* Open your eyes when you complete your intended time for abdominal breathing. Gently and mindfully transition to your next activity.

CLASS PRACTICE

- *Body scan and progressive muscle relaxation.* Perform a short body scan, followed by progressive muscle relaxation and then another short body scan.
- *Abdominal breathing.* Perform a set of 10 to 12 abdominal breaths.
- *Mindful standing and movement/yoga.* Stand in stillness for a minute or so before performing 10 to 15 minutes of mindful movements or yoga of your choice.
- *Breath and sound mindfulness.* Perform 20 to 30 minutes of breath mindfulness. Incorporate mindfulness of sounds

in the first few minutes. Stay aware of your experience of silence in the class.

- *Mindful seeing.* Contemplate something in your surroundings for a few minutes.
- *Mindful walking.* Do a few minutes of stretching and mindful walking.
- *Journal.* Describe your experience in detail, especially your experience with abdominal breathing. What did you notice? What will you do with this learning? You may want to consider continuing with the mindful consumption practices from last week and integrate another domain into your plan. Abdominal breathing can be done formally or informally anytime and anywhere. Begin with a set of 10 to 12 abdominal breaths and gradually increase the time and frequency. The more you practice it, the easier it becomes to breathe abdominally.
- *End of class.* Perform your chosen ritual to end the class.

THREE-PART BREATH

START THE CLASS

- Perform your start ritual.
- Take a few breaths, inhaling and exhaling fully and slowly.
- Gently close your eyes and come in touch with your intention to learn, experiment with, and practice mindfulness.
- Open your eyes and continue reading.

REVIEW YOUR PRACTICE

How is your practice going? Have you been in contact with your practice buddy? Have you done any abdominal breathing during the week? Have you chosen one more area of consumption to address and become mindful of? Are you more conscious and selective of what you eat, what you watch, what you read? Have you been aware of interacting mindfully with loved ones or others? Have you been saying "tell me more" when appropriate, showing your interest and curiosity in your loved ones or others? What object did you contemplate last week? Did you incorporate a period of silence into your practice? Have you been more mindful of what and how you eat? Have you been mindful of the sounds around you, and have you incorporated this into your mindfulness of the breath? Have you been walking mindfully? Contemplation and mindful walking can be integrated for rewarding results. How about yoga or mindful movements? Are you generally satisfied with your practice? If not, what do you need to modify or persist with in your current plan for another week?

CLASS READING

The *three-part breath* is also called *full breath* or *yogic breath*. It is a popular breathing technique. It engages the entire respiratory system and is believed to promote respiratory health and vitality. All three parts of the lungs (i.e., the low, the middle, and the upper parts) are filled with air in the inhalation and emptied of the air in the exhalation. Some teachers recommend that exhalation be in the order of the upper, middle, and lower parts of the lungs. Others do not emphasize such an order and recommend experimentation for what feels the most natural order of exhalation. With the help of the diaphragm, lungs are stretched in both the inhalation and the exhalation. It takes time and practice to clearly separate these three parts. The three-part breath is often described in terms of its three components and the importance of awareness of these components. In practice, however, it is one smooth and continuous process, with each part of the breath merging into the next until the inhalation and exhalation are complete. Three-part breath can be done while sitting, lying down, or standing. When sitting or lying down, follow these instructions:

- *Part 1. Breathing into the lowest lobes of the lungs—the belly area.* Place the hands on the abdomen and inhale deep into the belly, expanding the abdomen. Relax and exhale. (Repeat 5–10 times.)
- *Part 2. Breathing into the middle lobes of the lungs—the chest area.* Place the hands on the front of the lower rib cage, a few inches above the belly button, fingertips touching. Inhale into the abdomen and continue into the chest (notice the fingertips moving apart when the chest is rising and filled with air). Exhale. (Repeat 5–10 times.) Place the hands on the back of the rib cage and inhale. Notice the expansion of the chest from behind on inhalation. Exhale. (Repeat 5–10 times.)
- *Part 3. Breathing into the upper lobes of the lungs—the upper chest and neck area.* Place the hands on the top part of the chest right under the collarbones at the base of the neck. Inhale fully and notice the upper chest rising. If difficult to notice, breathe fully and deeply. After feeling the fullness of the breath, inhale a little bit more air before exhaling. Exhale. (Repeat 5–10 times.)

When standing, follow these instructions:

- *Part 1. Breathing into the lowest lobes of the lungs—the belly area.* Place the hands at waist level so that the fingers touch at the tips, palms of the hands toward the ground. Breathe in slowly and deeply into the belly, expanding the lower lobes of the lungs. Exhale fully. (Repeat 5–10 times.)
- *Part 2. Breathing into the middle lobes of the lungs—the chest area.* Place the hands on the chest, thumbs under the armpits and fingers touching at the tips, and palms toward the ground. Breathe in slowly and deeply, expanding the chest area and the middle lobes of the lungs. Exhale. (Repeat 5–10 times.)
- *Part 3. Breathing into the upper lobes of the lungs—the upper chest and neck area.* Place the hands on the back on the shoulder blades, side by side. The pinkies will be next to each other, arms close to or touching the ears, and elbows pointing upward to the sky. Breathe in slowly and deeply, expanding the upper part of the lungs. Exhale. (Repeat 5–10 times.)

CLASS PRACTICE

- *Abdominal breathing, body scan, and progressive muscle relaxation.* Lie down on the floor and make yourself comfortable. Begin by performing 10 abdominal breaths. Gently transition to performing a short body scan, followed by progressive muscle relaxation and then another short body scan.

- *Mindful standing and movement/yoga.* Stand in stillness for a minute or so before performing 10 to 15 minutes of mindful movements or yoga of your choice.
- *Three-part breathing.* Perform a set of 10 to 12 three-part breaths in your preferred position as described previously.
- *Breath and sound mindfulness.* Perform 20 to 30 minutes of breath mindfulness. Incorporate mindfulness of sounds in the first few minutes.
- *Mindful seeing.* Contemplate something in your surroundings for a few minutes.
- *Mindful walking.* Do a few minutes of stretching and mindful walking.
- *Journal.* Describe your three-part breathing experience in detail. What did you notice? Has the breathing exercise had any effect on the quality of your sitting meditation? What will you do with this learning? You may want to consider continuing with mindful consumption practices from the last 2 weeks and integrate another domain into your plan. Three-part breathing can be done formally or informally anytime and anywhere. A set of 10 to 12 breaths usually provides a sufficient amount of exercise. Do not strain your lungs.
- *End of class.* Perform your chosen ritual to end the class.

LESSON 15

RHYTHMIC BREATH

START THE CLASS

- Perform your start ritual.
- Take a few breaths, inhaling and exhaling fully and slowly.
- Gently close your eyes and come in touch with your intention to learn, experiment with, and practice mindfulness.
- Open your eyes and continue reading.

REVIEW YOUR PRACTICE

How is your practice going? Have you been in contact with your practice buddy? Have you done any abdominal breathing or three-part breathing during the week, formally or informally? Have you chosen one more area of consumption to address and become mindful of? Are you more conscious and selective of what you eat, what you watch, what you read? Have you been aware of interacting mindfully with loved ones or others? Have you been saying "tell me more" when appropriate, showing your interest and curiosity in your loved ones or others? What object did you contemplate last week? Did you incorporate a period of silence into your practice? Have you been more mindful of what and how you eat? Have you been mindful of the sounds around you, and have you incorporated this awareness into your mindfulness of the breath? Have you been walking mindfully? Contemplation and mindful walking can be integrated for rewarding results. How about yoga or mindful movements? Are you generally satisfied with your practice? If not, what needs to be modified? Or you can persist with your current practice a while longer before you make changes.

CLASS READING

Rhythmic breath is popular in part because of its intriguing implications for us as living beings in the universe. Everything vibrates, albeit with different frequencies, and the less solid an object, the higher it vibrates. For example, stones vibrate less than air. Vibration is the basis for change and transformation. Even what we may consider completely solid and unchangeable shifts, changes, and vibrates. Scientists have observed that matter changes all the time. There is rhythm in all change. Rhythm happens throughout the universe. Time is a function of this rhythm. The rhythm of the planets around the sun creates the passage of time: years, months, and seasons. Our bodies are governed by the law of rhythm. For the body to function well, we need to understand the need for regularity and harmony (Ladd, 2009; Ramacharaka, 1931). Rhythm is powerful. If the rhythm of a high-frequency sound is kept consistent, it breaks glass. The sound of a violin, if maintained long enough at a specific frequency, can break a bridge. This is why soldiers stop their rhythmic march when walking over bridges. Consistent, harmonious, and rhythmic motion of our fingers around a crystal glass makes music.

In rhythmic breathing, regular intervals between inhalation, holding, and exhalation are practiced. The longer the duration of the inhalation, the hold, or the exhalation, the more challenging and difficult rhythmic breathing becomes. One important recommendation is to always remember not to strain the lungs.

Some exercises encourage inhaling and exhaling with the same duration and have shorter breath holding (usually half as long) between inhalation and exhalation. Counting numbers internally is the usual method of estimating the duration. For example, inhale to the count of 6, hold to the count of 3, and exhale to the count of 6 (6:3:6), or the pattern could be 8:4:8, or 10:5:10, etc. Some exercises encourage regular but longer exhalation time than inhalation time—for example, 4:4:8. Some encourage regular and long durations of holding the breath between inhalation and exhalation—for example, 8:16:8. The more difficult and challenging the breathing patterns from increasing the duration of inhalation, exhalation, or holding, the longer it takes to develop the pattern as a regular practice. Experimentation is highly encouraged. Input from an experienced teacher might be necessary if you want to experiment with difficult rhythms. Kundalini yoga is one form of yoga practice that incorporates such breathing exercises. Professor Andrew Weil, MD, a well-known physician, author, and founder and director of the Arizona Center for Integrative Medicine, believes breath can be a powerful tool in reducing anxiety. In one of his audiotapes, he recommended a rhythm of 4:7:8 for rhythmic breathing (Weil, 2000).

Rhythmic breathing is a powerful way to increase mindfulness. In rhythmic breath, the main idea is to establish a rhythm while breathing. It is versatile and can be performed lying down, sitting, or standing. To do a basic 6:3:6 rhythmic breath, follow these instructions:

- Sit with a straight posture, neck aligned with spine, and chin tucked in slightly.
- Slowly inhale with a three-part breath, filling up the three parts of the lungs to the count of 6.
- Hold the breath to the count of 3.
- Slowly exhale, emptying the lungs to the count of 6.
- Notice that the rhythmic breath is a more conscious variation of the three-part breath.

Another way to establish rhythmic breathing is to use the rhythm of your own heartbeat. To do so, proceed as follows:

- Lie down in a comfortable position. Take a few mindful breaths, relaxing the body and the mind.
- Place your fingers on your pulse and count up to 6 beats several times, until the rhythm of your pulse becomes known to you.
- Practice using this rhythm in the inhale, starting with inhaling to the count of 6, holding to the count of 3, and exhaling to the count of 6.

CLASS PRACTICE

- *Three-part breath, body scan, and progressive muscle relaxation.* Lie down on the floor and make yourself comfortable. Begin by performing 10 three-part breaths. Gently transition to performing a short body scan, followed by progressive muscle relaxation and then another short body scan.

- *Mindful standing and movement/yoga.* Stand in stillness for a minute or so before performing 10 to 15 minutes of mindful movements or yoga of your choice.

- *Rhythmic breath.* Perform a set of 10 to 12 rhythmic breaths in your preferred position as described previously.

- *Breath and sound mindfulness.* Perform 20 minutes of breath mindfulness. Incorporate mindfulness of sounds in the first few minutes. Stay aware of periods of silence during the class.

- *Mindful seeing.* Contemplate something in your surroundings for a few minutes.

- *Mindful walking.* Do a few minutes of stretching and mindful walking.

- *Journal.* Describe your three-part breathing experience in detail. What did you notice? What will you do with this learning? Rhythmic breathing can be done formally or informally anytime and anywhere. A set of 10 to 12 breaths usually provides a sufficient amount of exercise. Do not strain your lungs. You may also want to consider continuing with mindful consumption practices from the last 2 weeks and integrate another domain into your plan.

- *End of class.* Perform your chosen ritual to end the class.

LESSON 16

ALTERNATE NOSTRIL BREATHING

START THE CLASS

- Perform your start ritual.
- Take a few breaths, inhaling and exhaling fully and slowly.
- Gently close your eyes and come in touch with your intention to learn, experiment with, and practice mindfulness.
- Open your eyes and continue reading.

REVIEW YOUR PRACTICE

How is your practice going? Have you been in contact with your practice buddy? Have you done any abdominal, three-part, or rhythmic breathing during the week, formally or informally? Have you chosen one more area of consumption to address and become mindful of? Are you more conscious and selective of what you eat, what you watch, what you read? Have you been aware of interacting mindfully with loved ones or others? Have you been saying "tell me more" when appropriate, showing your interest and curiosity in your loved ones or others? What object did you contemplate last week? Did you incorporate a period of silence into your practice? Have you been more mindful of what and how you eat? Have you been mindful of the sounds around you, and have you incorporated this awareness into your mindfulness of the breath? Have you been walking mindfully? Contemplation and mindful walking can be integrated for rewarding results. How about yoga or mindful movements? Are you generally satisfied with your practice? Do you want to persist with or modify your plan?

CLASS READING

Modern science has confirmed what yogis have known for several thousand years: We do not breathe equally from both nostrils. Typically, it is easier to breathe from one nostril than the other at any given point in time. The nostrils alternate throughout the day and night, anywhere from every 25 minutes to about every 3 hours. This is called the *nasal cycle,* and it has been studied in the West for the past 30 years. The nasal cycle was first described in the West by the German physician Richard Kayser in 1895 and is a physiological congestion of the nasal concha due to selective activation of one half of the autonomic nervous system. Scientists have studied the effects of the nasal cycle on the nervous system and the neuroendocrine, cardiovascular, and fuel regulatory hormone (insulin) systems (Block,

Arnott, Quigley, & Lynch, 1989; Klein, Pilon, Prosser, & Shannahoff-Khalsa, 1986; Shannahoff-Khalsa, 2007; Shannahoff-Khalsa, Boyle, & Buebel, 1991; Telles, Raghuraj, Maharana, & Nagendra, 2007). The research has suggested that the electrical activity of the brain is greater on the side opposite the open nostril. The flow of breath and energy from the left nostril is connected to the right-brain hemisphere and is associated with the parasympathetic nervous system. It can promote relaxation in the muscles and facilitate the attention turning inward. The flow of breath from the right nostril is associated with the left-brain hemisphere and with the sympathetic nervous system, which tends to activate, energize, and orient the organism to the outside.

The practice of controlled alternate nostril breathing is one of the most popular and basic breathing practices in the East (Rama, Ballentine, & Haynes, 2007; Ramacharaka, 1905; Saraswati, 2002). Harmonizing the two sides of the brain by alternate nostril breathing is believed to refresh, relax, and restore balance. Many practitioners and teachers use this technique prior to a sitting meditation to enhance their conscious experience. To perform alternate nostril breathing, take turns breathing from one of the nostrils in a rhythmic fashion. Various hand gestures are suggested in the literature to prevent flow of air from entering one or the other nostril. Some teachers do not provide any instructions and leave it up to the participant to find his or her own way. Alternate nostril breathing is typically performed in a sitting position. You can try the following:

- Bend your index and middle fingers so you have the thumb, the ring finger, and the pinky available to use. Close your right (RT) nostril with your RT thumb.

- Exhale fully and slowly from the left (LT) nostril, then inhale deeply and slowly from the LT nostril.
- Close the LT nostril with the pinky and ring finger of your RT hand, and release the RT thumb.
- Exhale from the RT nostril and inhale from the RT nostril.
- Close the RT nostril with the RT thumb, releasing the pinky and ring finger. Exhale from the LT nostril and inhale from the LT nostril.
- Continue to alternate the nostrils for the duration of the exercise. Begin with 10 rounds of breath and you may gradually increase to 5 or even 10 minutes.
- Choose a comfortable rhythm and maintain it throughout the exercise.

CLASS PRACTICE

- *Breath, body scan, and progressive muscle relaxation.* Lie down on the floor and make yourself comfortable. Begin by performing 10 three-part breaths. Use a comfortable and regular rhythm. Gently transition to performing a short body scan, followed by progressive muscle relaxation and then another short body scan.
- *Mindful standing and movement/yoga.* Stand in stillness for a minute or so before performing 10 to 15 minutes of mindful movements or yoga of your choice.
- *Alternate nostril breathing.* Perform a set of 10 to 12 rhythmic alternate nostril breaths.

- *Breath and sound mindfulness.* Perform 20 to 30 minutes of breath mindfulness. Incorporate mindfulness of sounds in the first few minutes. Maintain mindfulness of silence during the class.
- *Mindful seeing.* Contemplate something in your surroundings for a few minutes.
- *Mindful walking.* Do a few minutes of stretching and mindful walking.
- *Journal.* Describe your experience in detail. What did you notice? What will you do with this learning? Alternate nostril breathing can be done formally or informally. You can start with a round of 10 breaths and gradually increase the time to 3 to 5 minutes. Doing so can enhance the periods of sitting meditation, so consider incorporating it before your breath mindfulness. You may also continue to incorporate more areas of mindful consumption into your practice.
- *End of class.* Perform your chosen ritual to end the class.

CLEANSING BREATH

START THE CLASS

- Perform your start ritual.
- Take a few breaths, inhaling and exhaling fully and slowly.
- Gently close your and eyes come in touch with your intention to learn, experiment with, and practice mindfulness.
- Open your eyes and continue reading.

REVIEW YOUR PRACTICE

How is your practice going? Have you been in contact with your practice buddy? Have you done any abdominal, three-part, rhythmic, or alternate nostril breathing during the week, formally or informally? Have you chosen one more area of consumption to address and become mindful of? Are you more conscious and selective of what you eat, what you watch, what you read? Have you been aware of interacting mindfully with loved ones or others? Have you been saying "tell me more" when appropriate, showing your interest and curiosity in your loved ones or others? What object did you contemplate last week? Did you incorporate a period of silence into your practice? Have you been more mindful of what and how you eat? Have you been mindful of the sounds around you, and have you possibly incorporated this awareness into your mindfulness of the breath? Have you been walking mindfully? Contemplation and mindful walking can be integrated for rewarding results. How about yoga or mindful movements? Are you generally satisfied with your practice? If not, what needs to be modified?

CLASS READING

In *cleansing breath* (or *kapalbhati*), the breath is short, strong, and quick. The emphasis is on quick, forceful exhalation and natural, passive inhalation. The exhalation is done from the lowest part of the lungs with a quick, strong, and forceful contraction of the belly. No effort is put on the inhalation. When done correctly, the lungs are used almost like a pump expelling air out. The inhalation will automatically and effortlessly follow.

- Sit in a comfortable position with the back straight, the hands resting on the thighs.
- Inhale deeply, expanding abdomen. Then exhale through the nose, pulling in the belly with a quick and forceful

tightening of the abdominal muscles. The air is pushed out of the lungs by the contraction of the diaphragm.

- After exhalation, inhalation should not involve any effort. To inhale, just relax the abdominal muscles and the lungs will automatically expand and fill up with air.
- One can begin with a few breaths. A full round of kapalbhati includes anywhere from 15 to 21 breaths. Three rounds of kapalbhati are recommended before meditation. It is customary to breathe normally for a few seconds between the rounds.
- Be sure not to engage back or shoulders. The rapid breathing is done from the abdomen and not from the chest area.

Ancient yogic texts posit that cleansing breath cleanses the lungs and the respiratory system, increases the supply of oxygen, improves digestion, strengthens abdominal muscles, and increases energy for meditation and mental activity.

Bellows breath (a.k.a. *bhastrika*) is similar to the cleansing breath. The difference is that in bhastrika, both inhalation and exhalation are strong and forceful.

CLASS PRACTICE

- *Breath, body scan, and progressive muscle relaxation.* Lie down on the floor and make yourself comfortable. Begin by performing 10 three-part breaths. Use a comfortable and regular rhythm. Gently transition to performing a short body scan, followed by progressive muscle relaxation and then another short body scan.

- *Mindful standing and movement/yoga.* Stand in stillness for a minute or so before performing 10 to 15 minutes of mindful movements or yoga of your choice.

- *Cleansing breath.* Perform three rounds of cleansing breath.

- *Alternate nostril breathing.* Perform a set of 10 to 12 rhythmic alternate nostril breaths.

- *Breath and sound mindfulness.* Perform 20 to 30 minutes of breath mindfulness. Incorporate mindfulness of sounds in the first 5 minutes. Maintain mindfulness of silence during class.

- *Mindful seeing.* Contemplate something in your surroundings for a few minutes.

- *Mindful walking.* Do a few minutes of stretching and mindful walking.

- *Journal.* Describe your experience. What did you notice about cleansing breath? What will you do with this learning? Remember, cleansing breath is typically performed prior to a sitting meditation and prior to alternate nostril breathing.

- *End of class.* Perform your chosen ritual to end the class.

III

CULTIVATING COMPASSION

LESSON 18

THE RAIN APPROACH

START THE CLASS

- Perform your start ritual.
- Take a few breaths, inhaling and exhaling fully and slowly.
- Gently close your eyes and come in touch with your intention to learn, experiment with, and practice mindfulness.
- Open your eyes and continue reading.

REVIEW YOUR PRACTICE

How is your practice going? Have you been in contact with your practice buddy? Have you done any abdominal, three-part, rhythmic, alternate nostril, or cleansing breathing during the week, formally or informally? Have you chosen one more area of consumption to address and become mindful of? Are you more conscious and selective of what you eat, what you watch, what you read? Have you been aware of interacting mindfully with loved ones or others? Have you been saying "tell me more" when appropriate, showing your interest and curiosity in your loved ones or others? What object did you contemplate last week? Did you incorporate a period of silence into your practice? Have you been more mindful of what and how you eat? Have you been mindful of the sounds around you, and have you incorporated this awareness into your mindfulness of the breath? Have you been walking mindfully? How about yoga or mindful movements? Are you genuinely satisfied with your practice? Do you want to modify or persist with your plan?

CLASS READING

Mindfulness of Thoughts and Emotions

Throughout the book, I have encouraged awareness and acceptance of thoughts and emotions during mindfulness practice. Being mindful of thoughts and emotions means to accept and befriend them, to hold them with curiosity and kindness. Even negative, critical, and judgmental thoughts are held with kindness and friendliness. Similarly, troubling emotions, such as anger, fear, pain, and envy, are accepted and held with compassion. Accepting and befriending our thoughts and emotions can indeed be viewed as an act of self-compassion.

Judgmental thoughts and emotions can be the focus of mindful attention. This option becomes particularly helpful when, for example, a certain persistent thought or emotion demands your attention, making it difficult to practice breath, sound, or walking mindfulness.

In these instances, you may shift the focus of your attention from these other modes of mindfulness to the thought or emotion that is attracting your attention.

Becoming mindful of thoughts and emotions is similar to becoming aware of other events, such as breathing during mindful breathing, body sensations during a body scan, or listening to sounds during sound mindfulness. When you are mindful of your thoughts or emotions, you observe and witness them without getting caught up in the stories they may present. The witness, the "I" of your consciousness, the observer, contains your thoughts and emotions the same way the sky contains clouds or the ocean contains waves. We carefully note our thoughts and emotions; explore them with an attitude of curiosity; and hold them with compassion, kindness, acceptance, gentleness, and generosity. Keep in mind that thoughts and emotions come and go constantly, regardless of their content. Becoming aware of them enables us to further develop the ability to witness our experiences. This in turn takes us out of the "automatic pilot" of reactivity and provides the space we need to choose our response. In the same way we let go of one breath to keep our consciousness open to the next breath, we let go of thoughts or emotions to remain receptive to the next one.

Each part of the body has a job to do. The heart beats, the mind thinks and wanders, and the emotions are felt. With mindfulness, we become intimately aware and conscious of our mind habits and emotional habits. Mindfulness assists us in understanding and recognizing these habits. Thoughts and emotions are powerful distractors when you choose body sensations, breath, sound, or another focus as the anchor for your attention. Learning to be mindful of thoughts and emotions enhances, sharpens, and strengthens the ability to be mindful in general. This awareness enables us to see the mind and our emotions as just another facet of our humanity, a perspective that can free us from getting caught in their content. Witnessing and observing in this way will reduce our reactivity, shift us out of automatic-pilot mode, and provide more space to choose a response.

In my mindfulness class, one participant described her experience of mindful attention to thoughts and emotions in a stressful situation as follows:

> One of the biggest impacts mindfulness has had for me is changing my thoughts at work. In meetings where I might experience a sense of "too much to process" or "I can't do this" and normally have reacted defensively, I sometimes am able instead to breathe deeply, under the table to consciously open my clenched hands and just accept, to remember that I am not my mind and don't have to believe these thoughts, but instead, speak to myself with truth and love: "I am learning this new information, I am growing, I am not overwhelmed but enriched, this moment is as perfect as it can be." While I can't claim to do this all the time, it has made a tremendous difference, especially in this first year in a new job, new organization, new subject matter, and new colleagues.

RAIN

The RAIN approach is a practical and mindful way in which we can integrate and apply the two aspects of mindfulness—attention and compassion—to all experience, including thoughts and emotions. The acronym RAIN stands for recognition, acceptance, investigation, and nonidentification (Kornfield, 2008). You may choose to focus only on thoughts or only on emotions. Often, though, they are intertwined. With repeated practice, you will begin to discover how each comes and goes and interacts with others. When you attend to thoughts or emotions with mindful attention, you will discover that maintaining attention on them is as challenging as focusing on the breath, body sensations, or eating. For example, you may notice that the mind will wander away from focusing on thoughts. All along you have tried to focus on the breath and the mind wandered to thoughts. Now that you want to focus on thoughts, it goes to something else! Applying RAIN to thoughts and emotions helps us develop the ability to stand side by side with thoughts and emotions without reactivity.

To apply RAIN to thoughts, start with a few mindful breaths, bringing the attention inward. Then do the following:

- *Recognize the thought.* Become aware of the thought. If there is a particular thought that is asking for your attention, bring your full attention to that thought.
- *Accept the thought.* Receive it with kindness. Consider it a guest. Say hello and invite the thought in. Treat it well. Befriend your thought. Smile to the thought regardless of its content.
- *Investigate the thought.* Bring in an attitude of curiosity. Pay close attention to the various qualities of the thought. What kind of thought is here right now? Busy? Clear? Confused? Small? Large? Mild? Intense? Does it include images? What label could you give it, if any? Notice whether the thought is going along with a certain sensation in the body. Notice whether the thought is going along with a positive

or a negative emotional tone. Where in the body does it resonate the most? What are the sensations? Stay focused on the sensations for a time and note if they shift. Does the thought shift when the sensations shift? Notice that all thoughts arise, linger for a time, and then pass. Notice when one thought leaves and another thought arises. Notice their appearance and disappearance.

* *Nonidentify with the thought.* Treat each thought as a discrete event. Remind yourself that it is the job of the brain to have a stream of thoughts going through it at all times. Get to know your thoughts and the ways in which they come and go without getting lost in the story they tell.

Think of your awareness as the ocean and thoughts as waves on the ocean—waves that come and go, appear and disappear. Sometimes small waves come quickly, one after another. Sometime large waves come quickly. Sometimes there are only soft ripples. Sometimes there are slow but large currents. What kinds of waves are there on the sea of your awareness right now?

Or think of your awareness as the sky and the thoughts as clouds in the sky. Are there light, foamy clouds? Are there dark, thick clouds? Are there only patches? No matter how dense the clouds, they will eventually pass.

Or think of your awareness as the camera and your attention as the lens of the camera looking at a particular thought. Awareness is the operator that adjusts the lens of attention at will, choosing to go closer or farther away from the thought or to view it from a variety of angles.

These and other metaphors can be helpful reminders to disengage from a thought and remember the spaciousness of our awareness. Use of such metaphors remind us that thoughts are impermanent—they come, they linger, and they go—and that we can choose the manner of our engagement with them. We can observe them and allow them to be without entanglement. What metaphor resonates with you? Can you come up with others?

In my mindfulness class, one participant new to mindfulness felt that observing or witnessing thoughts and emotions was challenging and found the use of metaphors quite helpful. In particular, he was able to relate to the metaphor of the camera lens and said it was useful not only to adjust the lens, but also to adjust the noise level in his mind and quiet his thoughts with the knob!

To apply RAIN to emotions, start with a few mindful breaths, bringing the attention inward. Then do the following:

- *Recognize the emotion.* Now bring your attention to the feeling tone of this moment. Ask what is the emotional tone in this moment. Is it positive? Negative? Pleasant? Unpleasant? Neutral? What emotion is present?
- *Accept the emotion.* Receive the feeling with open arms. Be receptive. Consider it a welcome guest. Say hello to the emotion. Invite it in.
- *Investigate the emotion.* Stay curious. Explore it. What is here right now? Is it anger? Sadness? Boredom? Joy? Anxiety? Carving? Fear? Pick the emotion that is the most salient and calling the loudest for your attention. Pay close attention to its various qualities. Is it a warm feeling or a cold

feeling? Notice its size. Notice its intensity. Are there colors or images associated with this emotion? Use a label that best describes it. Notice whether there are sensations in the body that go along with these feelings. Notice whether there are thoughts that go along with the feelings. Like thoughts, emotions also come, linger for a time, and go. Notice how long the emotion lasts. What effect does this emotion have on your body? What sensations are you feeling? Where in the body do you feel it? Stay focused on those sensations. Breathe deeply as if into these sensations. When the body sensations pass, does the emotion change? Is another emotion featuring in your consciousness?

- *Nonidentify with the emotion.* Treat the emotion as a discrete event in the expanse of your awareness. Remind yourself that you are made to feel. Think of yourself as a feeling and thinking machine similar to 6 billion other human feeling and thinking machines in the world. It is nothing personal that you may experience a cascade of various emotions. This is your nature. It is part of your human condition. Accept that you are destined to feel and that this is not all there is to you. You are more than your thoughts and emotions.

The metaphors of ocean, sky, and camera lens are applicable here too. Get to know your emotions, and remember that your emotions do not have to dictate your response. Become aware of the tendency to react when emotions are present. This is where mindfulness can insert a pause in the habitual chain of reactivity. Note that when you become aware, you have the choice to respond rather than to react.

Practical Considerations for Your Weekly Plan

As mentioned previously, thoughts and emotions often go hand in hand. Extreme emotions, such as strong anger, fear, sadness, or cravings, can generate strong thoughts. Similarly, strong and persistent thoughts can generate emotions. For example, thoughts about the future can generate worries. Thoughts about a colleague can generate anger. Thoughts about the past can generate regret, sadness, or melancholy. Craving sweets can stimulate thoughts of our inability to postpone gratification.

To practice mindfulness of thoughts or emotions, the best approach to begin with is to choose a thought or an emotion that is not a source of great trouble. If you have had persistent thoughts about a subject for a long time or have had extreme emotions about a person or situation, those thoughts are not good starter practice items. For example, if fear is the emotion you would like to work on, begin your practice with something that produces mild fear. Similarly, if you would like to work on frustration or anger, begin your practice with a situation that produces mild anger or frustration. Take baby steps in the beginning of your practice.

Mindfulness of thoughts and emotions can be practiced formally and informally. During any sitting meditation, you may practice mindfulness of thoughts and emotions that arise in the context of that meditation. You might be practicing mindfulness of the breath, sensation in the body, sound, or mindful walking. When thoughts or emotions arise that you cannot easily let go of, you may apply RAIN to the thoughts or emotions and then return to the original practice.

If there are thoughts and emotions that you would like to address more specifically, then a more formal RAIN could be practiced and incorporated into your weekly plan. When you practice mindfulness of thoughts and emotions, you may find that RAIN begins to occur naturally and effortlessly. You may find that it becomes increasingly natural to apply RAIN in response to challenging thoughts or situations that arise during a typical day.

In my mindfulness class, one participant described how this practice influenced her in her daily activities:

> I was waiting in a long line to buy paint for a home project at the Home Depot around Christmastime after work. There was only one attendant mixing the paint, each order taking many minutes. I felt irritation rising in me as I waited. I also noted negative thoughts going through my mind, wondering why the store did not have more attendants. Normally, in similar situations, I would wait for a while and if not attended to, I would get angry, feeling my heart beating, blood boiling, sweating, or even shaking out of outrage. I then would complain to a manager, uttering disrespectful words about the store, and leave indignantly. The aftereffects of such a situation would last for several hours in my body—feeling tense, my mood feeling sour, and my thoughts negative, reviewing the situation over and over in my head and getting mad again and again. I would even feel more snappy at home, feeling impatient and tired, feeling sorry for myself, and would go to bed quickly after dinner cutting short the family time. By the next day I would be mad at myself for letting such a small thing ruin my day.

On this day, I chose a mindful approach. The minute I noted my heart beating faster I became aware that my irritation was already on the way to rise. I breathed deeply a few times and began to witness the course of my irritation. After less than a minute, I felt that the wave of irritation was beginning to subside. I noted that my thoughts were running a stream of commentary about expectations from business owners. I noted the thoughts and recognized that my "expectations" were running the show. I let go of the thought and began to notice the people around me and their reactions to the wait as if watching a movie. I could spot irritation and frustration in a few faces and chuckled at that. Then I brought my attention to the attendant who was mixing the various paints with great expertise. I noted his tired face. I marveled at his skill and consistency with which he was performing his work. When my turn finally arrived, I told the attendant about my admiration for his skills for mixing the paints and his evenness in performing his work. The tired attendant looked up at me, his eyes brightening and thanked me with a big, bright smile: "You made my day, lady. I now have energy for the rest of my shift." I left the store feeling uplifted and transformed by this small, yet for me, powerful, experience. The evening at home was splendid. I noted that mindfulness can make a difference in my life, my family's life, and the lives of others.

CLASS PRACTICE

- *Breath, body scan, and progressive muscle relaxation.* Lie down on the floor and make yourself comfortable. Begin by performing 10 three-part breaths. Use a comfortable and regular rhythm. Gently transition to performing a short body scan, followed by progressive muscle relaxation and then another short body scan.

- *Mindful standing and movement/yoga.* Stand in stillness for a minute or so before performing 10 to 15 minutes of mindful movements or yoga of your choice.
- *Cleansing breath.* Perform three rounds of cleansing breath.
- *Alternate nostril breathing.* Perform a set of 10 to 12 rhythmic alternate nostril breaths.
- *Mindfulness of thoughts and emotions.* Use your breath awareness as the anchor and apply RAIN when thoughts or emotions arise.
- *Mindful walking.* Do a few minutes of stretching and mindful walking.
- *Mindful seeing.* Contemplate something in your surroundings for a few minutes.
- *Journal.* What did you notice about your thoughts or emotions? What will you do with this learning? Incorporate mindfulness of thoughts and emotions into your mindfulness of breath practice. Incorporate mindfulness of thoughts and emotions informally throughout the day.
- *End of class.* Perform your chosen ritual to end the class.

LESSON 19

APPLICATION OF RAIN
TO FEAR AND ANGER

START THE CLASS

- Perform your start ritual.
- Take a few breaths, inhaling and exhaling fully and slowly.
- Gently close your eyes and come in touch with your intention to learn, experiment with, and practice mindfulness.
- Open your eyes and continue reading.

REVIEW YOUR PRACTICE

How is your practice going? Have you been in contact with your practice buddy? Have you been mindful of your thoughts or emotions? Have you done any breathing exercises during the week, formally or informally? Have you chosen one more area of consumption to address and become mindful of? Are you more conscious and selective of what you eat, what you watch, what you read? Have you been aware of interacting mindfully with loved ones or others? Have you been saying "tell me more" when appropriate, showing your interest and curiosity in your loved ones or others? What object did you contemplate last week? Did you incorporate a period of silence into your practice? Have you been more mindful of what and how you eat? Have you been mindful of the sounds around you, and have you possibly incorporated this awareness into your mindfulness of the breath? Have you been walking mindfully? Contemplation and mindful walking can be integrated for rewarding results. How about yoga or mindful movements? Are you generally satisfied with your practice? If not, do you want to modify or persist with your plan?

CLASS READING

Consider reviewing Lesson 18 if you feel you do not sufficiently remember that lesson.

Transforming Emotions

We do have the capacity to transform our emotions, even difficult emotions. To transform them, we have to first accept our role in creating them. We need to become increasingly mindful and conscious that emotions arise from within, not from without. Even if there are legitimate reasons why we may feel certain emotions in response to outside events, the sources of these emotions are within us nonetheless. That is the good news. When we become aware and recognize that emotions arise from within not without, then we are able to direct the light of mindful attention to them to facilitate their transformation.

Emotions are universal human experiences. Typically, negative emotions are experienced as unpleasant and positive emotions as pleasant. We desire and strive to increase the pleasant and decrease the unpleasant. This is part of our survival equipment. Desire keeps us eating, moving, having sex, going to work, and doing what is necessary to thrive. Desire can lead to difficulties when it becomes a craving and an obsession. Cravings and obsessions can control our lives in problematic ways. Addictions are an example of pleasure-seeking behaviors that take over. Addictions can even result in death. Similarly, the avoidance of the unpleasant can become problematic. Pain and sickness are not bad. They alert us to what is out of balance in the organism and actually can promote survival.

The mindful approach encourages us to accept and embrace all experience without censorship. To live life fully, we must make room for both the pleasant and the unpleasant experiences in our minds and hearts. When we pause, become still, and pay close attention to the nature of our experiences, we can engage in mindful inquiry rather than being controlled by attachment to the pleasant and aversion to the unpleasant. Desire, fear, anger, and their various shades can all have their place in our lives. It is not the emotions themselves; rather, it is the way in which we relate to our experiences that requires our mindful attention.

Similar to dealing with thoughts and emotions in general, we bring in the qualities of mindfulness, such as nonjudgment, gentleness, acceptance, curiosity, and beginner's mind, to the experience of various states, such as desire, pain, fear, or anger. Bringing conscious awareness and curious exploration to these states of the mind tends to reduce their grip and transform them.

All emotions, including negative emotions such as fear, anger, or physical pain, have had survival value for the human species. Mindful approaches to these emotions and states do not include trying to make them go away or disappear. Rather, the invitation is to consider changing our relationship to these emotions, sensations, and states of the mind.

Various emotions, including strong states such as desire, fear, or anger, are not the enemies. We embrace them for what they are. They stem from our life's energy. We recognize their value and their universality. And we can choose to transform our conscious relationship with them. Recognizing their importance, significance, and persistence does not mean that we let them run the show of our lives. We do not indulge in them. Nor do we suppress, seek to escape from, or deny their existence in ourselves or in others. Instead, we hold them in our consciousness mindfully. We hold them with a friendly or even loving attitude that recognizes that they are universal and impermanent and can be transformed.

In the mindful approach, our conscious awareness is called to witness emotions and to become the conductor of a magnificent orchestra in which each emotion represents a different and valued instrument. Imagine each emotion as a musical instrument. For a full and rich piece of harmonized and beautiful music, we need all of the instruments to produce their sounds. Certainly, the idea is not for one instrument to take over. When it does, the harmony and beauty of the music are lost. The idea is not to deny or disregard the sound of any of these instruments. The goal is by mindfulness, by our attention and compassion, to bring them together to play—balanced and harmonious. We humans are rich with a bounty of emotions; their nuances and shades make our lives rich and make each of us a unique being. The combination of emotions in each of us is a masterful piece of music. Mindfulness helps us to fine tune these instruments to create the best sound that they can make. We do not want to banish, break, or silence any of them. We accept ourselves fully. Tara Brach (2003), in her book *Radical Acceptance,* further explored these subjects beautifully.

Emotions come and go. They become a source of suffering when our identity and sense of self gets caught in them. When our mind is tangled with emotions, and our body produces tension and experiences stress in response to such emotions, our world becomes small and contracted. This is incompatible with life and true joy. When we free ourselves from this reactivity by practicing mindfulness, we remember the vastness of our being. We remember love and kindness and beauty and relatedness without denying our human nature. Freedom from emotions is not the absence of such emotions. Rather, it is when emotions arise but do not take over the sense of who we are. We continue to remember that we are larger than these transitory states and that such emotions come and go. We do not need to react or satisfy them unless we choose to.

The practice of RAIN is applicable here as well. We do the practice of RAIN on the bedrock of a general attitude of compassion and friendliness toward ourselves and our felt emotions.

Emotional Experiences Are Bidimensional

I have indicated that mindfulness practice and its development are best aided by attending to two aspects of mindfulness, a focused attention in the bedrock of a compassionate and an openhearted attitude. So far, we have mostly emphasized the specifics of focused attention. The second aspect of mindfulness—love, openheartedness, and compassion—has to do with the emotional valence and tone of our focused attention. Love and compassion can contain all emotions, including negative emotions such fear or anger. Negative emotions held in the energy of love, openness, and compassion will be transformed to either neutral or positive states of mind (Hanh, 2002).

Psychologists and researchers have long been investigating the role of positive and negative emotions on health and longevity. The psychological dimensions of health and illness have been well documented. It is clear that positive states of mind enhance health and longevity and that negative states of mind contribute to illness and disease (Chida & Steptoe, 2009, 2010; Danner, Snowdon, & Friesen, 2001; Kiecolt-Glaser, 2009; Segerstrom & Miller, 2004; Steptoe, Dockray, & Wardle, 2009).

Researchers have also found that most people believe that to feel good, you should no longer feel bad, and that to feel good, you must be free of pain, stress, and negative emotions. Over the years research has been accumulating that shows it is not necessarily so. For example, researchers at Arizona State University have demonstrated that there is a negative emotional system and a positive emotional system that work simultaneously and yet relatively independently of each other (M. C. Davis, Zautra, & Smith, 2004; Zautra, Affleck, Tennen, Reich, & Davis, 2005; Zautra, Davis, & Smith, 2004). They can be both up, both down, or one up and one down to various degrees. Can you think of an example that can engage both high positive and high negative emotions in you? Some people have reported that childbirth, getting married, or buying a home creates both high positive and high negative emotions. It is also common to have both high positive and high negative emotions in close and intimate relationships with loved ones such as mother, father, spouses, children, or partners. Winning a lottery or experiencing your child's great success can be examples of situations that promote mostly positive emotions. Car accidents, illness, or death are among the experiences that tend to result in mostly negative emotions. Neutral experiences, such as watching a TV program or brushing teeth, can be low in both positive and negative emotions. The relative independence of these two systems has an important implication for stress reduction: You can reduce stress not only by decreasing negative emotions but also by increasing positive emotions. Addressing problems or things that trouble us does not necessarily lead to positive emotions. We must also actively attend to, practice, and nurture positivity.

Mindfulness increases awareness of positive, neutral, and negative states and increases our ability to notice our felt experiences more fully. We begin appreciating much that could go unnoticed. Typically, we notice the absence and not the presence of what we are given. We take things for granted and forget their positive impact. For example, if we get a flat tire twice in a year, we generate negative emotions on both of those occasions. However, we do not generate any positive emotions on the other 363 occasions when we do not have a flat tire. We are not conscious of its positivity. We become acutely aware of our bodily sensations when we are sick or uncomfortable but rarely pay attention to our state of health and well-being. A mindful approach encourages awareness of the flat tire or lack thereof, sickness or health. It further encourages awareness of their respective negative or positive nature without reactivity.

Awareness of the positive and negative provides the opportunity to intervene in both areas: to increase the positive and to decrease the negative. This possibility for intervention can be a powerful asset for the individuals who suffer, for example, from chronic pain. Studies have challenged the premise that removal of pain is the only route to successful pain management (Zautra et al., 2005). With the use of various mindfulness techniques, the patients who are invited to reexamine pain and to learn to coexist with and accept their pain show improvement when simultaneously working on cultivating positive states. Surprisingly, the acceptance of pain and the work on increasing the incidence of positive states can result in reduction of pain perception itself. Patients who are assisted in finding fulfillment in spite of the pain eventually also report diminishment of pain. More broadly, mindfulness of virtually all experience has been shown to improve indications of health and well-being.

Despite this promise, however, expectations of such results from the outset may counter the beneficial effects. Expectations themselves function as a source of great stress (see Chapter 2).

Applying RAIN to Fear

To apply RAIN to fear, start with a few mindful breaths, bringing the attention inward. Then think of something that makes you afraid. Choose a fear that is troubling but not overwhelming.

- *Recognize the fear.* Notice the actual sensations in the body.
- *Accept the fear.* Say hello to it. Allow these sensations to be here. Make room for these feelings and sensations. Accept what is here. Allow and accept.
- *Investigate the fear.* Bring in genuine curiosity. Where is the fear located in the body? How large is it? What does it feel like? Is it a tingling, vibrating sensation or is it more like a hard solid lump? Are there any images associated with this fear? Is it associated with a color? What color(s) do you see? What thoughts are running through the mind? As you explore this fear, notice all the moment-to-moment changes. As you carefully explore and keep the gaze of your attention on this emotion, like all experience, you may notice the experience of fear changes constantly.
- *Nonidentify with the fear.* Notice the changes and entertain the possibility of a more objective, nonpersonal relationship with this fear, considering it as *fear*—not *my fear.* Fear is a universal experience. Expand your consciousness around this fear. Remind yourself of the vastness of your being. See your fear in the context of your entire being. See yourself in the context of your neighborhood, town, country, Earth, the galaxy, and the universe.

Ideally and with practice, when real-life situations arise that stimulate the emotion of fear in you, you will be able to invoke and engage a mindful inquiry and response rather than reactivity, when applicable. That is, you will only protect yourself from a real danger, not an imagined one. Fear is hardwired in our nervous system. Fear is a given. Indeed, if a car was about to hit you, or a wild animal to attack you, the best thing to do would be to run. Such an evolutionary message is designed to promote survival. It is not a mistake! And yet, so many of the things that we fear are not a real threat. The hypothetical situations and the worst-case scenarios that we create in our minds, which provoke fear and anxiety, are so often merely the product of our thoughts. If you strip the layers from any fear, you will likely find the fear of nonexistence at the core. This is fear arising from the impermanence of one's life. It is driven by the fragility of life and our certain departure from life. When we become reactive in the face of our fears, we can become locked in to the biochemistry of the stress response—fight, flight, and freeze. The state of fear reactivity is incompatible with life and joy. Fears come and go. Fear becomes suffering when our identity and sense of self is caught in it, when our mind is tangled in fear and our bodies tight with it, our world becomes small and contracted. We forget the vastness of being. We forget love and kindness and beauty and relatedness.

Freedom from fear is not the absence of fear. Rather, it is what happens when fear arises without taking over our sense of who we are. When we are afraid, it helps to remember that we are larger than our fear, and the threat posed by it is usually only a ripple or a wave in an ocean. We accept fear and its existence, but we also put it in perspective. In time, as each wave rolls in, we will not forget the ocean. We are calmed knowing that the ocean is vast, that it is filled with waves of all shapes and sizes, and that all waves come and go. Cultivating mindfulness gives us the ability to hold our fears in perspective and with tenderness without sacrificing our freedom to a enjoy life.

Applying RAIN to Anger

Anger is an emotion. It is energy. It is natural. Similar to fear, it has its own wisdom and intelligence as a part of our survival equipment with which we are born. Anger need not be suppressed. We do not need to get rid of the energy that comes with strong emotions. Rather, we need to look at our relationship to these emotions. When the energy of anger arises, it could be a signal to turn the attention from the object (what is out there) to the subject (our self).

Anger is an energy that we need to hold with tenderness and compassion. The energy of anger comes from within, not without. Each time we experience the energy of anger, we can engage the energy of mindfulness, compassion, and loving-kindness, which can serve as antidotes. We first bring the attention to the anger, make room for it, and take care of it. Thich Nhat Hanh (2002) stated that anger is like a crying baby to whom we must pay attention. The energy of mindfulness can transform the energy of the anger. He said the rays of the sun shine on, circulate around, and penetrate the flower. The flower opens up to the energy of the sun. So, too, mindfulness does not merely circulate around the anger; it penetrates the anger and opens it up to transformation.

The energy of anger has some danger if not cared for mindfully. It can turn to rage, hatred, or violence. With the energy of anger, we can lose lucidity. Lama Surya Das's (2007) application of RAIN identified the following steps to mindful anger management:

- acknowledge/experience/feel it,
- allow the presence of anger,
- reflect/analyze/scrutinize/cradle it,
- recognize its impermanence, and/or
- respond (not react).

Response to anger could be one or a combination of the following:

- letting go,
- responding constructively and or creatively, and
- calling on the energy of loving-kindness and compassion.

Thich Nhat Hanh (2002) said that when angry, simply bring your attention to mindful breathing, breathing in "I know I am angry," breathing out "I am taking good care of my anger." By doing this, you embrace your anger with the energy of mindfulness; this alone will transform the energy of anger. To neglect anger is to leave a hungry and crying child unattended—it will cry louder.

One participant in my mindfulness class felt that the application of mindfulness had been greatly helpful in managing his road rage. He described his example of improvement and transformation this way:

> I was driving in a heavy snow in heavy traffic on a two-lane street. I was driving in the right lane, which abruptly came to

an end due to snow piled up on the side. I needed to get to the left lane, the only remaining lane to go forward. I started the indicator and patiently waited for the proper moment to change my lane, and after a time very slowly began to move to the left. The car in the left lane began to honk ceaselessly, denying me entrance to the lane, and began to pass by. The driver looked enraged and was showing me his middle finger with much intensity and emotion. I felt a surge of strong energy in my body. I noted that my heart was beating fast, I was feeling warm, and my breath had become shallow, irregular and fast. I took a deep breath. Then another one. I quickly realized that I had to pay attention and take care of the sensations I was feeling. I inhaled and exhaled fully and slowly. Gaining composure, I finally got into the left lane. As I drove forward there came a sense of "sorrow" for the angry driver. How stressed and ashen he looked. His face was tight with anger. His body language was tense with hostility and agitation. I knew how unpleasant those states were and how terrible the mind and the body feels. I actually felt a sense of compassion and sadness for him. I even laughed, remembering the absurdity of him showing me his middle finger. How odd and absurd. What was that supposed to do? I returned my attention to my breath again, which had become more regular and quiet. The sensation of heat was gone and my heart was beating normally. I felt OK. I did not feel any inclination to go after that car and aggress back.

CLASS PRACTICE

- *Breath, body scan, and progressive muscle relaxation.* Lie down on the floor and make yourself comfortable. Begin by performing 10 three-part breaths. Use a comfortable and regular rhythm. Gently transition to performing a short body scan, followed by brief progressive muscle relaxation and then another short body scan.

- *Mindful standing and movement/yoga.* Stand in stillness for a minute or so before performing 10 to 15 minutes of mindful movements or yoga of your choice.
- *Cleansing breath.* Perform three rounds of cleansing breaths.
- *Alternate nostril breathing.* Perform a set of 10 to 12 rhythmic alternate nostril breaths.
- *Mindfulness of thoughts and emotions—apply RAIN to a fear or to anger.* Use your breath awareness. Bring a situation to mind that creates some fear or some anger. Be sure to choose a situation that brings about a manageable (mild to low moderate) level of emotion. Apply RAIN as was described in the section Applying RAIN to Fear. Modify accordingly to apply to anger or other difficult emotions. Review Lesson 18 for practice recommendations.
- *Mindful walking.* Do a few minutes of stretching and mindful walking.
- *Mindful seeing.* Contemplate something in your surroundings for a few minutes.
- *Journal.* What did you notice about applying RAIN to difficult thoughts or emotions? What will you do with this learning? Incorporate the application of RAIN into your week informally as much as possible. Practice RAIN in response to emotions that arise throughout the day. Informal practice will prepare you for real-life situations and help even during strong emotions.
- *End of class.* Perform your chosen ritual to end the class.

CULTIVATING POSITIVE STATES

START THE CLASS

- Perform your start ritual.
- Take a few breaths, inhaling and exhaling fully and slowly.
- Gently close your eyes and come in touch with your intention to learn, experiment with, and practice mindfulness.
- Open your eyes and continue reading.

REVIEW YOUR PRACTICE

How is your practice going? Have you been in contact with your practice buddy? Have you been mindful of your thoughts or emotions? Have you attempted to apply RAIN to fear or anger? Have you done any breathing exercises during the week, formally or informally? Have you chosen one more area of consumption to address and become mindful of? Are you more conscious and selective of what you eat, what you watch, what you read? Have you been aware of interacting mindfully with loved ones or others? Have you been saying "tell me more" when appropriate, showing your interest and curiosity in your loved ones or others? What object did you contemplate last week? Did you incorporate a period of silence into your practice? Have you been more mindful of what and how you eat? Have you been mindful of the sounds around you, and have you incorporated this awareness into your mindfulness of the breath? Have you been walking mindfully? How about yoga or mindful movements? Are you generally satisfied with your practice? If not, what needs to be modified? Or do you need to persist with your plan a while longer?

CLASS READING

Buddha once said that there are 10,000 doors to dharma, meaning that there are unlimited ways in which we can become enlightened. Similarly, there are many ways in which positive states can be cultivated.

Noticing the Ordinary

Mindful attention increases our ability to notice our felt experiences more fully. We begin appreciating much that could go unnoticed. Typically, we notice the absence, not the presence, of what we are given. We take things for granted and forget their positive impact. The importance of practicing gratitude—the recognition of and thankfulness for what we are given and already have—has been recognized in almost all religions for thousands of years (Walsh, 1999). Robert Emmons (2007) and his colleagues have researched the topic for many years and have linked gratitude to health and well-being. To enhance and notice the ordinary, you can make a list of all the experiences that give you a sense of joy or pleasure in your journal. Keep adding to the list. Each time you experience even the most subtle sense of joy, write it down and answer the following questions:

- What was it that gave you joy? Example: "As I was walking on the campus, I noted a beautiful flower and smelled it."
- Were you aware of your experience while it was happening? Example: "Not right away, but when I noticed the sweet smell, I became aware that I was enjoying the experience."
- What were the sensations in your body? Example: "I felt lightness in the chest, shoulders relaxed, mouth smiling, sensations of air going through my nose, warmth on my face, recognizing the sweet smell."
- What was the mood/feeling? Example: "Joy, lightness, pleasure, pleasantness, carefree feeling."
- What thoughts were going through your mind? Example: "This flower is beautiful. I wish I could stay outside. Maybe I should take the day off and go on a nature walk. There are many flowers that I pass by without noticing them. I should note this in my journal."

Smiling

We smile and laugh when we feel good. Smiling is a visual sign of happiness, signaling inward feelings of joy. Researchers have found that the act of laughter and smiling itself, regardless of the under-lying feelings, can have a positive effect. It triggers the endorphin activation, increases resistance to pain, improves the work of the immune system, and enhances health and well-being (Devereux & Heffner, 2007; Gorman, 2011; Miller & Fry, 2009; Provine, 2000; Strean, 2009; Wolf, 2005). Smiling and laughter signal acceptance and have an impact on communication with others. Most represen-tations of the Buddha depict him with a smile. Thich Nhat Hanh emphasized the act of smiling in his teachings. He reminded us that if smiling happens when we feel joyful—that is, conscious smiling—even in the absence of felt joy it will assist us in cultivating such a state. He further said that sometimes your joy is the source of your smile, but sometimes your smile can be the source of your joy.

To practice smiling, note the frequency of your smiling. Note the situations during which you smile naturally and those during which you do not smile. Make a conscious effort to increase the frequency and situations in which you smile. Smile when alone or when nothing is happening, and note the subtle shifts in your inner experiences. Make smiling part of all your meditative activities. Make an effort to incorporate smiling during your sitting, walking, breathing, and lying-down practices.

The Four Rivers of Life

Dr. Angeles Arrien is an anthropologist, teacher, and organizational consultant. In her book *The Second Half of Life: Opening the Eight Gates of Wisdom*, Arrien (2007) said that many ancient cultures and societies believed that for a joyful life, we need to stay connected with, and open to, the forces of inspiration, challenge, surprise, and love. She used the word *river* to refer to these forces. If we do not stay connected to these sources/forces/rivers, our life's energy will become blocked and stagnated, and we will become the "walking dead," experiencing soul loss, depression, lack of zest, animation, and vitality or other negative manifestations.

Inspiration is about being in touch with our dreams, creativity, and creative fire. It is about recognizing when we are uplifted and feel a sense of expansion. It means being open to and in touch with our sense of hope and inspiration. To stay fully alive, we must stay connected to the fire in our belly.

Challenge invites us to stretch and grow beyond our comfort zone; to not rely solely on what is familiar; and to explore new possibilities, interests, and domains—to go beyond and let go of any fixed notion of who we are and what we are capable of. To stay fully alive, we must be willing to be challenged and take on challenges.

Surprise requires that we trust what comes our way while we stay fluid, flexible, and curious. It invites us to examine our attachments and preconceived notions and challenges us to let go of the ones that no longer serve us. It asks us to make room for the creative and generative forces of life.

Love touches the deepest layers of our being and keeps us connected to our deepest expressions of humanity. Without it, our hearts begin to close and our vitality shrivels.

I have used these concepts in my classes to highlight the possibility of redefining day-to-day experiences in life-affirming rather than self-defeating terms. They can be helpful in integrating complex emotional experiences. Mindfulness is awareness. The four rivers increase our awareness of how we define and therefore experience life circumstances. Often, life circumstances do not easily lend themselves to positive or negative definitions. Rather, we find ourselves with an array of mixed experiences. For example, challenge will not necessarily feel positive. If we accept that challenge is one of the powerful forces that keep us connected to life, we can learn to value and welcome it, to see that challenge is one of the powerful forces that makes our life rich and exciting. This interpretation can help redefine a variety of experiences that might otherwise produce negative emotional states, such as fear and stress. The new project that our boss puts on our lap unexpectedly (surprise), and for which we may not be fully prepared, will no longer feel like a threat; rather, it could be viewed as an expansion of our current state (challenge), could engage our creativity (inspiration), and could even foster a sense of service (love).

With awareness of these four important life forces, we are more likely to allow ourselves to feel surprised and touched by a nice e-mail that arrives during a busy day. We do this by just taking a moment to acknowledge and experience the good feelings that might have otherwise gone unnoticed. This awareness can also engage our creativity and love when we respond to it from the heart.

When we take notice of the flow of these four rivers in our daily life and notice these important connections to life and life force, how it moves through us and how it is manifested, we can experience a sense of "wow" rather than "ouch."

One word of caution is warranted here. These concepts do not easily lend themselves to cases of habitual risk-taking and excitement-seeking behaviors or pathological manic states, which require professional assessment and treatment.

To put the four rivers to work, whenever possible, set aside a few minutes at the end of each day. Review the day and see if you can become aware of a situation that you could highlight or redefine using the four rivers. In your journal, you may want to answer the following questions:

- What has inspired me today?
- What has challenged me today?
- What has surprised me today?
- What has touched me today?
- Is there anything I can redefine now? Did anything happen today that I did not take notice of? Did I react negatively to anything that could have been viewed in a more positive light?

Indeed, the Buddha teaches us that in life whatever or whomever comes our way is a teacher. We need not look at anyone or anything as the enemy; rather, we must realize that this person or situation has come about to teach us a lesson. Our job is find out what it is that we need to learn, and to find out the point of the lesson for our own growth, development, and well-being.

CLASS PRACTICE

- *Breath, body scan, and progressive muscle relaxation.* Lie down on the floor and make yourself comfortable. Begin by performing 10 three-part breaths. Use a comfortable and regular rhythm. Gently transition to performing a short body scan followed by brief progressive muscle relaxation and then another short body scan. Incorporate smiling into your practice.

- *Mindful standing and movement/yoga.* Stand in stillness for a minute or so before performing 10 to 15 minutes of mindful movements or yoga of your choice. Incorporate smiling into your practice.
- *Cleansing breath.* Perform three rounds of cleansing breath.
- *Alternate nostril breathing.* Perform a set of 10 to 12 rhythmic alternate nostril breaths.
- *Sitting meditation/mindfulness of breath.* Perform 20 to 30 minutes of breath mindfulness. Incorporate smiling into your practice. Remain mindful of silence during the class.
- *Mindful walking.* Do a few minutes of stretching and mindful walking.
- *Mindful seeing.* Contemplate something in your surroundings for a few minutes.
- *Sound.* Incorporate mindfulness of sounds in your sitting or walking meditation.
- *Journal.* Reflect on the day and think about ordinary situations that you may now consider in a positive light. Reflect on situations in which you noticed even a subtle sense of joy and pleasure. Reflect on situations that you might have experienced negatively, and now look at them in a different light on the basis of your understanding of the four rivers. Journal about them. You can use the questions that were listed in this lesson for your reflections and journaling. What have you learned from this lesson about cultivating

positive states? What will you do with this learning? Consider making a list of what is pleasant and enjoyable to you and continue to add to it during the week. Note subtle experiences. Make note of ordinary things and situations that you become aware of. Smile as much as possible. Apply the four rivers to your day-to-day experiences.

- *End of class.* Perform your chosen ritual to end the class.

BEHOLDING

START THE CLASS

- Perform your start ritual.
- Take a few breaths, inhaling and exhaling fully and slowly.
- Gently close your eyes and come in touch with your intention to learn, experiment with, and practice mindfulness.
- Open your eyes and continue reading.

REVIEW YOUR PRACTICE

How is your practice going? Have you been in contact with your practice buddy? Have you been mindful of your thoughts or emotions, including difficult emotions such as fear or anger? Have you been more aware of your positive experiences? Have you been able to see the extraordinary in the ordinary? Have you attempted to reflect on difficult experiences and redefine them? Have you done any breathing exercises during the week, formally or informally? Have you chosen one more area of consumption to address and become mindful of? Are you more conscious and selective of what you eat, what you watch, what you read? Have you been aware of interacting mindfully with loved ones or others? Have you been saying "tell me more" when appropriate, showing your interest and curiosity in your loved ones or others? What object did you contemplate last week? Did you incorporate a period of silence into your practice? Have you been more mindful of what and how you eat? Have you been mindful of the sounds around you, and have you incorporated this awareness into your mindfulness of the breath? Have you been walking mindfully? How about yoga or mindful movements? Are you generally satisfied with your practice? If not, what do you need to modify? Or do you want to continue with your plan a while longer?

CLASS READING

Beholding is a way of transforming difficult emotions into a positive experience, particularly in interpersonal situations. I have used similar processes in group situations as an introduction to the development of compassion toward others, followed by more traditional methods—that is, loving-kindness (see Lesson 22), tonglen (giving and receiving; see Lesson 23), and forgiveness (see Lesson 24).

- *Pleasant person.* You may begin by sitting in a meditative posture, bringing your attention inward and taking a few

mindful breaths. Think of someone you really care about—
your child, a child you know and love, a dear friend. Imagine this person vividly. Let pleasant colors, scents, and
sounds come to mind in connection with the image. Stay
with the pleasant image for a couple of minutes. Smile if
you would and note the sensation in the body, the quality
of the mind, and the quality of the heart.

• *Difficult person.* Next, think of someone you dislike or with
whom you are upset or annoyed. (Choose someone who
does not generate hatred or strong anger. Do not choose a
particularly difficult situation. Choose something in the
medium range.) Bring into mind the situation in some
detail. Stay with this for a couple of minutes. Note the sensations in the body, the quality of the mind, and the quality
of the heart. What differences do you experience in your
bodily sensations, mind, and heart in the two experiments?

• *Recognize the difficult person's shared humanity.* Think of
the person in vivid terms, as you know them now. In the
images, include sight, sound, texture, and other details and
attributes that bring this person to life in your mind. As
you look at this person, remind yourself that he or she
shares the same human condition with you. For example:

  • In life, the person has loved and lost as you have.

  • The person has experienced pain, anxiety, and fear as
    you have.

  • The person has been angry and irritated as you have.

  • The person has experienced joy and sadness as you
    have.

- The person has been unfair as you have.
- The person has been misunderstood as you have.
- The person has been betrayed as you have.
- The person has betrayed others as you have.
- The person is imperfect and has many faults as you have.
- The person is beautiful, magnificent, and awesome in his or her human form as you are.
- It is like looking into the mirror; note that by the virtue of being human, you both share similar life experiences. Your stories might be different, but your human experiences are not.
- *Embracing the difficult person's vulnerability.* Try to cultivate friendly feelings toward this person. Smile at this person. Think of this person as a newborn infant or a very frail elderly person. Imagine either of these scenarios with vivid details. Remind yourself that the person is also vulnerable to illness, old age, and death. Continue to smile and remain friendly. Bring forth feelings of benevolence toward this person as best you can. Allow yourself to experience compassion, love, and tenderness toward this person.

Practice of Beholding

Practice the previous steps with as many people as possible. The next time someone stimulates your negative emotions, remind yourself of the person's vulnerabilities and your shared humanity. Look at the person and see him or her as human, with the same set of emotions, thoughts, and experiences as yours. Bring forth feelings of love and compassion for the person in the same way that you would want to be seen and loved. Be the love you want to experience. More specifically:

- *See the person.* Truly notice the person as a human being. Notice his or her complex and intricate features.
- *Notice your thoughts.* Notice the thoughts that might be coming up. Notice whether various judgments are present. Pay attention and remain genuinely open to any prejudices, judgments, or likes or dislikes that may come up. Whatever thoughts or judgments are present, they are welcome. Acknowledge your thoughts without self-criticism, and bring your attention back to the person before you.
- *Notice your feeling tone.* Notice the feeling tones that might be present. Are they generally pleasant, unpleasant, or neutral? Acknowledge the feeling tone without evaluation or self-criticism.
- *Shared humanity.* As you look at this person, remind yourself of your shared humanity and that this person also feels sorrow, joy, pleasure, anger, sadness, anxiety, worry, and irritation. We all share the universality of our human condition—whether we are man, woman, or child; short, tall, fat, or thin; blue eyed or brown eyed; blonde or dark haired—we all are in this life together.
- *Shared vulnerability.* Remind yourself that the person is also vulnerable to sickness, old age, and death. Think of the person as a baby, a young child, or a frail elderly per-

son. Remind yourself of his or her fragility and of the impermanence of all experience.

- *Compassion and love.* Now bring forth feelings of benevolence or even feelings of love and compassion toward the person, and wish the person well.

Beholding in a Group

Beholding can also be a group activity. When done in groups, this guided contemplation includes gazing into a classmate's eyes while the leader recites statements describing the fragility, impermanence, and the universality of human experience. This activity is typically experienced as initially difficult and awkward and eventually as intimate, intense, powerful, and eye opening. Laughter and tears are invariably present. The pairings are switched every 2 to 3 minutes until all group members get a chance to gaze at each other. Eventually, the exercise includes an invitation to invoke an immediate experience of love and compassion for another. Needless to say, leading such an exercise requires experience and expertise on the part of the leader.

One participant in my mindfulness class, a long-time practitioner of meditation and spiritual development, recalled going to a country fair with his family and becoming aware of the endless stream of judgments he experienced for every person he encountered there. He related that many of the judgments were unflattering and negative. Noticing the manner in which the endless judgments arose helped him see that the negative thoughts were inconsistent with his deeper desire to be compassionate and open to others. Through the practice of forming kinder thoughts, he was able to feel more ease, less guarded, and more benevolent toward others. The key was the choice to maintain kinder thoughts while continuing some awareness of the negative thoughts arising and passing in the background. At the end of the course, and when reflecting with the group on his experience, he tearfully described how moved he was by the realization that compassionate orientation to others can be a choice. And the choice, once made, can be uplifting and powerful. He said, "In the past, thinking on how to be compassionate to others, I never realized that it can be a mere matter of choice. It is just amazing to me and still hard to believe!"

CLASS PRACTICE

- *Breath, body scan, and progressive muscle relaxation.* Lie down on the floor and make yourself comfortable. Begin by performing 10 three-part breaths. Use a comfortable and regular rhythm. Gently transition to performing a short body scan, followed by brief progressive muscle relaxation and then another short body scan.
- *Mindful standing and movement/yoga.* Stand in stillness for a minute or so before performing 10 to 15 minutes (or longer) of mindful movements or yoga of your choice.
- *Cleansing breath.* Perform three rounds of cleansing breath.
- *Alternate nostril breathing.* Perform a set of 10 to 12 rhythmic alternate nostril breaths.

- *Beholding.* Apply the beholding exercise as described previously.

- *Mindful walking.* Do a few minutes of stretching and mindful walking.

- *Sound.* Incorporate mindfulness of sounds in your sitting or walking meditation.

- *Mindful seeing.* Contemplate something in your surroundings for a few minutes.

- *Journal.* Write about your experience of beholding. What have you learned? What will you do with this learning? Be sure to incorporate beholding in your weekly plan.

- *End of class.* Perform your chosen ritual to end the class.

LOVING-KINDNESS

START THE CLASS

- Perform your start ritual.
- Take a few breaths, inhaling and exhaling fully and slowly.
- Gently close your eyes and come in touch with your intention to learn, experiment with, and practice mindfulness.
- Open your eyes and continue reading.

REVIEW YOUR PRACTICE

How is your practice going? Have you been in contact with your practice buddy? Have you practiced beholding? Have you felt a sense of compassion for yourself or others? Have you been mindful of your thoughts or emotions, including difficult emotions such as fear or anger? Have you been smiling? Have you been aware of your pleasurable and enjoyable experiences, albeit subtle ones? Have you attempted to redefine difficult life experiences? Have you done any breathing exercises during the week, formally or informally? Have you chosen one more area of consumption to address and become mindful of? Are you more conscious and selective of what you eat, what you watch, what you read? Have you been aware of interacting mindfully with loved ones or others? Have you been saying "tell me more" when appropriate, showing your interest and curiosity in your loved ones or others? What object did you contemplate last week? Did you incorporate a period of silence into your practice? Have you been more mindful of what and how you eat? Have you been mindful of the sounds around you, and have you possibly incorporated this awareness into your mindfulness of the breath? Have you been walking mindfully? How about yoga or mindful movements? Are you generally satisfied with your practice? If not, what do you need to modify? Or would you rather continue with your current practice a while longer?

CLASS READING

Why Loving-Kindness?

Loving-kindness and compassion are popular anchors of meditation in Buddhism. In Pali, a Middle Indo-Aryan language that is the language of the earliest Buddhist scripture, they are called *metta* and *karuna,* respectively. The two are among the four sublime states or immeasurables. The other two states are sympathetic joy (*mudita*) and equanimity *(upekkha).* The four immeasurables, including loving-kindness and compassion, are considered necessary to maintain an accepting and nonjudgmental attitude toward difficult sensations, thoughts, or emotions.

Loving-kindness meditation is recommended to the Buddha's followers in the 2,500-year-old Pali Canon. A different set of practical instructions, still widely used today, is found in the 5th century CE Visuddhimagga. Other variations on this traditional practice have been popularized by contemporary teachers such as Pema Chodron (2001), Sharon Salzberg (1995), and Jack Kornfield (2007, 2008).

Loving-kindness is a very specific feeling. It is a selfless caring for the well-being of another regardless of the person's personal attributes or behavior. This practice helps the individual to refrain from being offensive, bitter, and resentful and instead to develop a mind of friendliness, accommodativeness, and benevolence that seeks the well-being and happiness of others.

Loving-kindness is considered an antidote to negative attitudes and emotions. It helps us to cultivate positive emotions and to let go of ill will and resentment. Negative attitudes and emotions such as hostility, anger, cynicism, fear, confusion, closed heart, and frustrated expectations for others are all sources of stress. Cultivating and directing feelings of empathy, compassion, warmth, tenderness, and love toward self and others helps to dissolve such negative attitudes. Research has produced strong support for compassionate practices in promotion of health and well-being (Coffey, Hartman, & Fredrickson, 2010; Fredrickson, Cohn, & Finkel, 2008; Goetz, Keltner, & Simon-Thomas, 2010; Hofmann, Grossman, & Hinton, 2011; Lutz, Greischar, Perlman, & Davidson, 2009).

In the Theravada Buddhist tradition, the loving-kindness begins with the meditator cultivating loving-kindness toward himself or herself, then teachers or other revered individuals, loved ones such as family members, neutral people or strangers, difficult people or even enemies, and finally all sentient beings. This practice uses repeated phrases, images, and feelings to evoke the spirit of loving-kindness and friendliness. Specifically included are phrases addressing freedom from hostility, resentment, and anger; freedom from pain and physical suffering; freedom from mental suffering, distress, anguish, or anxiety; and a wish to live happily and conduct life with ease and happiness. This practice can be a part of a formal sitting practice or used informally, when a situation arises. It can be done lying down, standing, or even moving about.

There are no limits on the number of individuals toward whom we might direct loving-kindness. Similar to the gradual progression between these stages, it is recommended to use a graduated sequence within each stage as well. For example, choosing individuals who bring about strong emotions, positive or negative, is not recommended during the early stages of this practice. Rather, a gradual progression is needed to maintain the even, impartial, and heartfelt feelings of well-being and thoughts of love toward those for whom we have harbored strong emotions. For example, it is not recommended to begin by picking a loved one for whom we have strong sexual feelings or a difficult person for whom we have strong feelings of rage or anger. Rather, the teaching is to select those for whom we can maintain the impartial loving feelings and gradually include those for whom we have strong feelings as long as we can maintain the heartfelt, impartial, and deep feelings of welfare and love. With persistence and in time, many practitioners will be able to expand the scope of their loving-kindness practice.

At first, this practice can feel mechanical, simplistic, or awkward. It may feel like a religious prayer or may even bring about feelings of impatience, frustration, or irritation. If you experience negative emotions in response to this practice, it is especially important to hold these emotions with a kind and gentle attitude. Whatever arises in you should be held in the spirit of loving-kindness.

Loving-Kindness Practice

To do a loving-kindness meditation, first relax and take a few mindful breaths. Bring forth tender and warm feelings, then inwardly recite loving-kindness phrases. Below is a suggested set of phrases that I use in my classes. They can be adjusted in any way that would enhance the experience of this practice for you to make it more authentic, genuine, and heartfelt. In addition, sometimes it helps to put your hand on the region of the heart during this meditation.

Self. Imagine yourself vividly. Picture yourself as you are now. If you think it will help you conjure up tenderness toward yourself presently, think of yourself as a baby or a child held in love and tenderness. Smile at your own image and give your body the message of joy and ease. Bring tenderness and love to this image. When you have brought about such feelings of love and tenderness toward yourself, recite the statements below or any variations that work for you:

- May I be free from anger, resentment, or hatred.
- May I be filled with compassion and kindness.
- May I be safe and protected from pain and suffering.

- May I be peaceful.
- May I live with ease and be free.

Benefactor. When ready, allow your own image to fade away and bring your attention to visualizing a teacher or a benefactor—someone toward whom you have a sense of ease and uncomplicated and unconditional love and regard. Now picture this person vividly, and direct your tender feelings of love and caring by reciting your own or the following statements:

- May you be free from anger, resentment, or hatred.
- May you be filled with compassion and kindness.
- May you be safe and protected from pain and suffering.
- May you be peaceful.
- May you live with ease and be free.

Loved one. Next, visualize a loved one—someone you really care about but for whom you do not have romantic or sexual feelings. Imagine this person vividly, and when you feel ready, direct your own or the following statements toward him or her:

- May you be free from anger, resentment, or hatred.
- May you be filled with compassion and kindness.
- May you be safe and protected from pain and suffering.
- May you be peaceful.
- May you live with ease and be free.

A neutral person. Next, bring to mind someone neutral, someone for whom you do not have either positive or negative feelings.

Bring tenderness, love, and caring toward this person. When ready, recite your own or the following statements toward him or her:

- May you be free from anger, resentment, or hatred.
- May you be filled with compassion and kindness.
- May you be safe and protected from pain and suffering.
- May you be peaceful.
- May you live with ease and be free.

A difficult person. Now think of someone who has been difficult for you. In the beginning, think of someone who does not readily bring about intense or overwhelming negative emotions, but rather someone with whom you have had mild or moderate difficulty. Bring the person to mind vividly, and direct tender and loving feelings toward him or her. Sometimes it can help thinking of this person as a very young child or a frail elderly person to bring to heart tender feelings. When ready, recite your own or the following statements toward him or her:

- May you be free from anger, resentment, or hatred.
- May you be filled with compassion and kindness.
- May you be safe and protected from pain and suffering.
- May you be peaceful.
- May you live with ease and be free.

All beings. When ready, visualize your entire household, neighborhood, city, state, country, continent, the whole Earth and beyond, in all directions. Then recite your own or the following statements toward all beings:

- May all beings be free from anger, resentment, or hatred.
- May all beings be filled with compassion and kindness.
- May all beings be safe and protected from pain and suffering.
- May all beings be peaceful.
- May all beings live with ease and be free.

When you open your eyes and move out into the world with the spirit of loving-kindness, as you walk down the street, sit in traffic, in the office, or in line at the store or the movie theatre, you can offer loving-kindness in a silent and simple way to people that you encounter. This offering will connect you with people all around you. It will help quiet your mind and open your heart.

One participant in my mindfulness class used loving-kindness to overcome deep-seated resentment he held toward his mother. He was an educated and successful 40-year-old man who had harbored years of resentment and anger toward her because of humiliations that he had felt in his late adolescence. She had made him ashamed repeatedly and had insulted him for his lack of achievements in high school. Although he had not thought of these incidents for some time, he had never fully forgotten them either. Sending heartfelt wishes of well-being toward her and seeing her as a vulnerable human being enabled him to truly let go of the past. He stated that he allowed tenderness to move through him as if washing over the past grievances that were not a "big deal" after all. He began to see these memories through the eyes of a 40-year-old rather than a 17-year-old. He later related to the class that in his last visit with his parents, he was able to hug his mother with a true spirit of love, tenderness, and ease.

CLASS PRACTICE

- *Breath, body scan, and progressive muscle relaxation.* Lie down on the floor and make yourself comfortable. Begin by performing 10 three-part breaths. Use a comfortable and regular rhythm. Gently transition to performing a short body scan, followed by brief progressive muscle relaxation and then another short body scan.
- *Mindful standing and movement/yoga.* Stand in stillness for a minute or so before performing 10 to 15 minutes (or longer) of mindful movements or yoga of your choice.
- *Cleansing breath.* Perform three rounds of cleansing breath.
- *Alternate nostril breathing.* Perform a set of 10 to 12 rhythmic alternate nostril breaths.
- *Loving-kindness meditation.* Apply loving-kindness meditation as described previously.
- *Mindful walking.* Do a few minutes of stretching and mindful walking.
- *Sound.* Incorporate mindfulness of sounds in your practice.
- *Mindful seeing.* Contemplate something in your surroundings for a few minutes.
- *Journal.* Describe your experience in detail, especially your experience with the loving-kindness meditation. What did you learn? What will you do with this learning? Be sure to incorporate compassion-building practices with a focus on loving-kindness meditation in your weekly plan.
- *End of class.* Perform your chosen ritual to end the class.

GIVING AND RECEIVING (TONGLEN)

START THE CLASS

- Perform your start ritual.
- Take a few breaths, inhaling and exhaling fully and slowly.
- Gently close your eyes and come in touch with your intention to learn and practice mindfulness.
- Open your eyes and continue reading.

REVIEW YOUR PRACTICE

How is your practice going? Have you been in contact with your practice buddy? Have you practiced loving-kindness meditation or beholding? Have you felt a sense of and awareness of compassion for yourself or others? Have you been able to invoke compassion for yourself and others with more ease? Have you been smiling and taking note of enjoyments, even simple and subtle ones? Have you attempted to redefine difficult experiences? Have you been mindful of your thoughts or emotions, including difficult emotions such as fear or anger? Have you done any breathing exercises during the week, formally or informally? Have you chosen one more area of consumption to address and become mindful of? Are you more conscious and selective of what you eat, what you watch, what you read? Have you been aware of interacting mindfully with loved ones or others? Have you been saying "tell me more" when appropriate, showing your interest and curiosity in your loved ones or others? What object did you contemplate last week? Did you incorporate a period of silence into your practice? Have you been more mindful of what and how you eat? Have you been mindful of the sounds around you, and have you possibly incorporated this awareness into your mindfulness of the breath? Have you been walking mindfully? How about yoga or mindful movements? Are you generally satisfied with your practice? If not, what do you need to modify? Or do you want to continue with your current plan a while longer?

CLASS READING

Giving and receiving (or *tonglen*) is a practice of developing compassion (Chodron, 2001; Kasl, 1999; Rinpoche, 2002). *Tonglen* is a Tibetan word that means "sending and taking." This practice is emphasized in Tibetan Buddhists traditions. Similar to loving-kindness meditation, giving and receiving has become popular in the West because of its simplicity and power. This practice has been attributed to the great Indian teacher Atisha Dipankara Shrijnana, born in 982 CE and arriving in Tibet in the 11th century.

In this practice, one visualizes taking into oneself the suffering of others on the in-breath, and giving happiness and success to others on the out-breath. It can be practiced formally or informally when the situation arises. Several variations to this practice exist. The one I use in my classes is detailed as follows:

- Choose a quiet, private place.
- Make yourself comfortable.
- Calm the mind with a few minutes of mindful breathing.
- When ready, bring to mind the last person with whom you felt anger or conflict.
- Keep your eyes closed, and imagine this person is standing or sitting directly in front of you. Get in touch with the anger or conflicted emotions, feeling your emotions, thoughts, conclusions, and judgments around that anger. Note the sensations in the body.
- Let go and take a few mindful breaths.
- Bring the person to mind again. Imagine that this person, too, carries suffering and anger inside. The anger and suffering fills this person's body in the form of a black, tarry smoke. Imagine that you can see right through this person's skin and see that cloud of black smoke. Imagine that you can smell it, almost feeling the texture of this smoke.
- Now, imagine you can see a vent between this person's eyes and between your eyes, as if you both have a vent in the area of the third eye. On the inhalation, imagine that you

are inhaling to draw a stream of this smoke out of this person's vent toward yours and that the stream of smoke then enters into the vent between your eyes. The smoke comes into you, travels down to your heart, and becomes filtered and transformed into a beam of white light. Then, on your exhalation, send this beam of white light of loving-kindness from your heart directly into this person's heart.

- Do this for several breaths. In the inhalation, draw black smoke of suffering from this person's third-eye vent into yours. The smoke is filtered in you and is transformed into the bright light of loving-kindness. In the exhalation, send this beam of loving-kindness from your heart to the person's heart.

- Now, take the nature of this person's suffering and get in touch with its universality. Many, many people suffer in this same way. Bring them to mind—those whom you know and those millions and millions whom you will never meet but who also suffer in this way. Breathe in all of that suffering throughout the planet, and send an unlimited number of beams of white light to all these suffering people.

- End of practice: Gently open your eyes and prepare for the next activity.

Many of my class participants have reported feelings of lightness, joy, and release after our group practice of giving and receiving. They typically find this exercise powerful and eye opening. They feel closer to and compassionate about each other without specific knowledge of their life stories. A teacher of mindfulness, an attorney, once told me that he used giving and receiving in an important and tense meeting at work during which the two sides had to come to an agreement on some 20 or more items of dispute. Much was at stake for both sides, financially and politically. The attorney of the opposing side appeared defensive, hostile, imposing, intimidating, and uncompromising. He described the following:

> I simply reminded myself that he (the attorney of the opposite side) must be suffering. He has anger, irritation, and much negative emotion and feeling inside. His arrogance surely must be hiding deep fears. On the inhale I tried to breathe in the thick dark smoke of negative emotions from him, bringing in his negativity and filtering it in my heart and in breathing out, sending him the filtered bright light of loving-kindness—from my heart to his. I kept doing it throughout the meeting. There was a shift in the tone of the meeting at some point from tense and hostile to a more cooperative, negotiating, and compromising position. At the end, we were able to agree on all but two points. The meeting was considered a success by all accounts.

CLASS PRACTICE

- *Breath, body scan, and progressive muscle relaxation.* Lie down on the floor and make yourself comfortable. Begin by performing 10 three-part breaths. Use a comfortable and regular rhythm. Gently transition to performing a short body scan, followed by brief progressive muscle relaxation and then another short body scan.
- *Mindful standing or movement/yoga.* Stand in stillness for a minute or so before performing 10 to 15 (or more) minutes of mindful movements or yoga of your choice.

- *Cleansing breath.* Perform three rounds of cleansing breath.
- *Alternate nostril breathing.* Perform a set of 10 to 12 rhythmic alternate nostril breaths.
- *Giving and receiving.* Apply giving and receiving as described previously.
- *Mindful walking.* Do a few minutes of stretching and mindful walking.
- *Mindful seeing.* Contemplate something in your surroundings for a few minutes.
- *Journal.* Describe your experience in detail, especially your experience with the giving-and-receiving meditation. What did you notice? What will you do with this learning? Be sure to incorporate compassion-building practices with a focus on giving and receiving in your weekly plan.
- *End of class.* Perform your chosen ritual to end the class.

FORGIVENESS

START THE CLASS

- Perform your start ritual.
- Take a few breaths, inhaling and exhaling fully and slowly.
- Gently close your eyes and come in touch with your intention to learn, experiment with, and practice mindfulness.
- Open your eyes and read the below.

REVIEW YOUR PRACTICE

How is your practice going? Have you been in contact with your practice buddy? Have you practiced giving and receiving, loving-kindness meditation, or beholding? Have you felt a sense of and awareness of compassion for yourself or others? Have you been able to invoke compassion for yourself and others with more ease? Have you been smiling and taking notice of your pleasant experiences? Have you redefined any difficult experiences? Have you been mindful of your thoughts or emotions, including difficult emotions such fear or anger? Have you done any breathing exercises during the week, formally or informally? Have you chosen one more area of consumption to address and become mindful of? Are you more conscious and selective of what you eat, what you watch, what you read? Have you been aware of interacting mindfully with loved ones or others? Have you been saying "tell me more" when appropriate, showing your interest and curiosity in your loved ones or others? What object did you contemplate last week? Did you incorporate a period of silence into your practice? Have you been more mindful of what and how you eat? Have you been mindful of the sounds around you, and have you possibly incorporated this into your mindfulness of the breath? Have you been walking mindfully? How about yoga or mindful movements? Are you generally satisfied with your practice? Do you think you want to modify or continue with your current practice plan?

CLASS READING

> Hatred does not cease by hatred. Hatred ceases by love alone. This is the eternal law.
>
> —The Buddha

> If we could read the secret history of our enemies we should find in each man's life sorrow and suffering enough to disarm all hostility.
>
> —Longfellow

Why Forgiveness?

Cultivating positive emotions such as compassion, loving-kindness, and forgiveness is not solely an altruistic undertaking. The practice of cultivating positive emotions also enhances our own health and well-being by reducing stress and improving the functions of several bodily systems, including the cardiovascular, endocrine, and immune systems (Bono, McCullough, & Root, 2008; Coffey Hartman, & Fredrickson, 2010; Danner, Snowdon, & Friesen, 2001; Davidson et al., 2003; Emmons, 2007; Fredrickson, Cohn, & Finkel, 2008; Friedberg, Suchday, & Srinivas, 2009; Kiecolt-Glaser, 2009; Lawler-Row, Karremans, Scott, Edlis-Matityahou, & Edwards, 2008; Pace et al., 2009; Steptoe, Dockray, & Wardle, 2009; Tugade, Fredrickson, & Feldman Barrett, 2004; Xu & Roberts, 2010). The eight positive emotions of love, awe, hope, compassion, faith or trust, forgiveness, joy, and gratitude are considered important factors in relief and protection from stress by regulating the neuroendocrine system (Vaillant, 2008).

Forgiveness is a universal concept. Nearly all wisdom traditions and religions, such as Hinduism, Buddhism, Judaism, Christianity, and Islam, incorporate notions of compassion and forgiveness in their teachings (Walsh, 1999).

Forgiving is a conscious choice to let go. When we forgive, we let go of resentment, anger, revenge, and obsession. In time, we may not only let go of anger and resentment, but we also may be able to cultivate positive feelings toward those who have harmed us. That is, forgiveness enables us to reduce and eventually eliminate negative emotions, as well as to cultivate and increase positive ones.

Forgiveness does not justify actions of the wrongdoer. Nor does it mean that we will trust those who have harmed us or allow them to hurt us again. It does not mean that we will necessarily reconcile with them either or even tell them about our own internal process. Forgiveness is a movement of the heart to let go of the burden of the past pain, resentment, anger, and outrage that has kept us trapped and held us hostage. It is an act of courage (Kornfield, 2002, 2007, 2008).

Robert Enright, professor of psychology at the University of Wisconsin at Madison, is an expert in using forgiveness as a form of therapy and education. In his book *Forgiveness is a Choice* (Enright, 2001), he provided a detailed account of the work done by him and his research group over a 15-year period. He demonstrated that forgiveness can reduce anxiety and depression and increase self-esteem and hopefulness. According to Enright, forgiveness that is approached sensitively, systematically, and properly will benefit the forgiver more than the forgiven. It will decrease negative emotions and bring about clarity and peace.

For most people, forgiveness is a process. With deep wounds, the work of forgiving can take a long time, and professional help might be required. Various stages may surface, such as grief, rage, sorrow, fear, or confusion. In the end, we allow ourselves to feel the pain and to release it through forgiveness. Forgiveness is fundamentally for our own well-being. It liberates us from holding on to the negativity that stops us from being who we really are, the negativity that constricts and contracts our lives and our being. Releasing the sorrows of the past allows our hearts to open and enables us to move on.

Practice of Forgiveness

In Buddhist practices, Jack Kornfield tells us, forgiveness is tradi-
tionally sent in three directions: toward the harm that we have done
to others, toward the harm that we have done to ourselves, and
toward the harm that has been done to us. In each direction, it is
important to choose those areas of wounding that are not overwhelming. Rather, it is recommended to assume a gradual approach
and, with practice, to gently and progressively move to the more
sensitive areas.

To do a forgiveness meditation, start with a few mindful breaths,
bringing the attention to the area of the heart. Connect with a sense
of tenderness within. Smiling or putting your hand on the region of
the heart can be helpful in becoming present to this experience. Now
we begin asking and extending forgiveness in three directions.

- *Forgiveness for harm we have done to others.* First, reflect
  on, remember, and visualize a time or times when you physically, emotionally, or spiritually hurt or harmed others by
  your words, actions, or thoughts, knowingly or unknow-
  ingly. Take your time and let yourself remember. With this
  remembering, note the sensations in the body. Sense the
  pain you might be feeling and any feelings of shame, disappointment, sadness, anxiety, and fear. Allow and experience the pain, sorrow, or regret. Stay with and be present
  to your experiences and gently whisper:

  > I have caused pain and suffering to others by my
  > words, actions, or thoughts. I have caused them

pain and suffering, knowingly or without knowing. I have lied to, neglected, hurt, betrayed and abandoned others. This was because of my fears, anger, pain, hurt, or confusion. I ask for forgiveness. Forgive me for the pain and suffering that I have caused.

- *Forgiveness for harm that we do to ourselves.* When ready, gently move to the second direction of the practice. We now focus on forgiving ourselves. We have caused ourselves pain and suffering, knowingly or without knowing. We have hurt, harmed, betrayed, or abandoned ourselves with our words, actions, or thoughts. Let yourself remember, picture, and feel the ways in which you have been harsh, unkind, and mean to yourself, have acted against yourself, or have harbored harmful thoughts about yourself. Feel the pain, sorrow, and regret. Take your time and allow yourself the feelings that you have. Stay present to your experience, to your mind and heart, while gently whispering:

    I have caused myself pain and suffering by my words, actions, or thoughts. I have caused pain and suffering, knowingly or without knowing, because of my fears, anger, pain, hurt, or confusion. I have lied to, neglected, hurt, betrayed, and abandoned myself. I ask for forgiveness. I offer myself forgiveness. I forgive myself.

Add to or modify these statements on the basis of your own life experiences to make them more specific to your situation.

- *Forgiveness for the harm that others have done to us.*
  When ready, gently move to the third direction of the
  practice. This is forgiveness for those who have caused us
  pain and suffering, knowingly or without knowing, by
  their words, actions, or thoughts. Think of a person or a
  situation of pain and hurt that you can experience without
  becoming overwhelmed by the feelings and sensations.
  Use a gradual approach. Begin with areas of pain and hurt
  that are not very troubling and gradually work your way
  up. Let yourself remember, picture, and sense the pain you
  still carry from this situation or the person. Allow yourself
  to experience whatever that brings up. You can now
  release yourself from this burden by extending your forgiveness if you are ready. Breathe gently in the area of the
  heart, whispering:

  > You have caused pain and suffering by your words,
  > actions, or thoughts. You have lied to, neglected,
  > hurt, betrayed, or abandoned me. You have caused
  > pain and suffering, knowingly or without knowing,
  > because of your fears, anger, pain, hurt, or confu-
  > sion. I forgive you. (Note: If you are not yet ready to
  > forgive, you may offer your intention to forgive.)

  Add to or modify these statements on the basis of
  your own life experiences to make them more specific to
  your situation.

Repeat these three directions of forgiveness as many times as
you need to or until you can experience a release in your heart. Be

gentle and soft. At times, you may not feel a release but only the burden or anguish you carry. Forgiveness is difficult. It can take time. It cannot be artificial or forced. It is opening up to our own vulnerability. It is accepting life as is. It is accepting fear, loss, grief, injustice, and disappointment. It is accepting the full range of human nature in ourselves and in others.

One participant in my mindfulness class, who was visibly moved by the experience of forgiveness meditation, shared with the class that he included his only sister in his forgiveness meditation, from whom he had been long estranged. He had harbored much resentment toward her during the process of caring for their elderly parents until their death over 25 years ago. He and his sister had strong disagreements regarding the care of their parents during this time. Over the years, his sister had contacted him a few times, but he had evaded true contact and connection. Now, for the first time in 25 years, he thought of his sister in the process of meditation for forgiveness. He tearfully recalled many good times and realized how much he missed his only sibling. The following week, he returned to class and announced that he had contacted his sister. For the first time in 25 years, they visited, reunited, and embraced each other. He was grateful for the practice of forgiveness and felt that without it, he would not have been able to summon the courage he needed to contact his sister and would not have experienced the heartfelt sense of healing, warmth, and closeness that he deeply needed.

Some experts would argue that the act of forgiveness is not complete until we can wish those who have hurt and harmed us well. In other words, we not only need to forgive but also to want well for those who have hurt or harmed us. It is possible then to do forgiveness meditation/reflections and then to take it a step further and cultivate good feelings and thoughts by loving-kindness meditation and directing a part of the loving-kindness toward those who have hurt or harmed us or toward those whom we may consider our enemies. We build this level of forgiveness and benevolence gradually and with sensitivity and care for our own needs and feelings in the process. We may find that this is not a straight line. There will be days on which we may feel more receptive and ready than other days. Or we may find that a new dimension of the same situation or person will require reworking.

CLASS PRACTICE

- *Breath, body scan, and progressive muscle relaxation.* Lie down on the floor and make yourself comfortable. Begin by performing 10 three-part breaths. Use a comfortable and regular rhythm. Gently transition to performing a short body scan, followed by brief progressive muscle relaxation and then another short body scan.

- *Mindful standing and movement/yoga.* Stand in stillness for a minute or so before performing 10 to 15 minutes (or longer) of mindful movements/yoga of your choice.

- *Cleansing breath.* Perform three rounds of cleansing breath.

- *Alternate nostril breathing.* Perform a set of 10 to 12 rhythmic alternate nostril breaths.

- *Forgiveness.* Perform a forgiveness meditation as described previously.

- *Mindful walking.* Do a few minutes of stretching and mindful walking.
- *Mindful seeing.* Contemplate something in your surroundings for a few minutes.
- *Journal.* Describe your experience in detail, especially your experience with forgiveness. What did you learn? What will you do with this learning?
- *End of class.* Perform your chosen ritual to end the class.

BRING IT ALL TOGETHER: A MINDFUL DAY

Every few months, or even more regularly, plan a mindful day that you will conduct in silence. The purpose of such a day is to cultivate stillness and awareness and to deepen your practice. It will be a day to slow down and to attend to yourself. You can invite one or more like-minded people to join you. Shop for and prepare some food mindfully ahead of time or incorporate mindful cooking into your day. During the time you have set aside for your mindful day, maintain silence and open yourself to nondoing and the simplicity of being, such as sitting, walking, listening, seeing, eating, cleaning, stretching, and attending to and being aware of these states. Minimize expectations. Incorporate nature into the day as much as possible. Particularly during walking and contemplation, nature can powerfully connect you to the universe at large. Have only your journal with you and possibly a very small selection of meaningful and awe-inspiring poems. Let go of phones, cell phones, computers, e-mails, other reading materials, or other means of communications. Bring along a nonjudgmental attitude, beginner's mind, and openness to whatever may arise during the day, including boredom, guilt, anxiety, or restlessness. You may consider the following sequence. Please note that the length of suggested practices are simply recommendations. You may adjust according to the knowledge of your own practice. This is a day to be with your senses, thoughts, and emotions and to befriend all of your experiences and states.

A MINDFUL DAY

- Begin with your start ritual and clarify your intention for the day.
- Breath exercises—three-part breathing (that incorporates abdominal and rhythmic), followed by alternate nostril breathing (15 minutes)
- Progressive muscle relaxation (15 minutes)
- Body scan (15 minutes)
- Mindful movements/gentle yoga (1 hour)
- Sitting meditation (45 minutes)
- Bio break (for restroom, drinking water, etc.) and stretch (15 minutes)
- Nature walk—mindful walking, mindful listening to sounds, and contemplation (30–45 minutes to 1 hour)
- Lunch—mindful eating, followed by a brief rest period (1 hour, or longer if you are preparing your meal)
- Sitting meditation (30 minutes)

- Stretch/light yoga (15 minutes)
- Forgiveness meditation (15 minutes)
- Loving-kindness meditation, incorporating beholding and giving and receiving (20 minutes)
- *Journal.* What I have learned? What will I do with my learning? When will I do another mindful day? What would I shift, modify, change for my next mindful day?
- End with your chosen ending ritual.

CONCLUDING REMARKS

Mindfulness is simple and yet not easy! Practiced regularly, it reduces stress. Striving for results and expectations, however, paradoxically reduces its effectiveness. It requires compassion and discipline. Practice is the key. You must have a clear intention to learn and practice and to set aside time and a place to facilitate practice development. Planning and journaling will assist you in doing so. Be specific and detailed in your planning and journaling. Enrolling others or joining a community of like-minded practitioners will be extremely helpful in keeping you on track with your practice. Find a community of others who are willing to join in. Do not get discouraged when you procrastinate. Procrastination is a human attribute; recognize, accept, and investigate your procrastination and remain nonjudgmental. Start over immediately without indulging in self-criticism, belittling your accomplishments, or downplaying the importance of the practices.

I am reminded of a story that I heard a long time ago. There was an intelligent person, a genius, who decided to become a mathematician. He studied mathematics and became a mathematician in a short time. Then he decided to become an astronomer. He studied astronomy for a time and succeeded in becoming one. Then he decided to become a swimmer. He studied intently and drowned! Mindfulness is very much like swimming. It has to be practiced, not just studied.

I think of mindfulness as a way of maintaining mental hygiene that is very similar to maintaining dental hygiene. To keep the teeth and gums healthy, you have to brush your teeth regularly. There may very well be various theories behind how and why it is necessary to brush teeth, who came up with the idea first, what toothbrush or toothpaste to use, and how long to brush. However, these underpinnings do not concern the practitioner of tooth brushing each morning. The practice of mindfulness, regardless of its philosophical origins, can keep the mind brushed, healthy, and resilient and, as such, exert a powerful impact on other bodily systems. The work is never finished. You do not stop brushing your teeth because you did it all last week. You do not take long breaks from brushing because you feel tired or do not like tooth brushing. Or, if you took a break and missed several times, you do not say that because you missed several times it is of no use to brush your teeth anymore. You persist, in spite of interruptions or inconsistencies, because you believe dental health is important. You practice and accept dental hygiene as a part of day-to-day life. You do not debate it. Most likely, the lessons your parents gave you to instill the regular habit of tooth brushing did not work overnight. Your learning took trial and error and persistence. Thomas Moore (2003), in his book *The Soul's Religion,* quoted Sheng-yen, a Zen master:

> Be soft in your practice. Think of the method as a fine silvery stream, not a raging waterfall. Follow the stream, have faith in its course. It will go its own way, meandering here, trickling there. It will find the grooves, cracks, and crevices. Just follow it. Never let it out of your sight. It will take you. (p. 255)

In summary, to develop your practice of mindfulness: Be clear about your intention, make time, make place, pay attention, be gentle, start over, journal, find a community, release self-defeating thoughts, and enjoy yourself.

Mindfulness is all about self-care and activation of powerful self-healing abilities that are invested in the magnificent and complex biology of the human form. Establishing regular practice can be a struggle, no doubt. But pressing on to an eventual embrace of a daily practice can mean an extraordinary adventure with boundless rewards.

Sometimes we need to reevaluate the way in which we set priorities. All too often, I have heard the following:

> These practices are great. When I do them I see the difference. But I do not have time to practice regularly. There are so many things I need to do (or I must do). There are not enough hours in the day. Most days by the time I want to practice I am too tired.

We probably set our priorities on the basis of what feels important and urgent. Important and urgent matters, no doubt, go at the top of our to-do lists. Unimportant and nonurgent matters go at the bottom of our to-do lists. I think we lose track of practice when we put urgent but unimportant ahead of nonurgent but important matters. Development of a sustaining mindfulness practice, most likely, will not feel urgent initially. Yet it is a very important way to enhance your well-being. You can choose to put it on your daily "to-be" list.

ADDITIONAL RESOURCES

Following is a select list of books, audio CDs, DVDs, magazines, and websites that you may find helpful as you explore mindfulness and meditative practices. Please note that additional classes, retreats, readings, and multimedia resources are increasingly available all over the world. Online search tools such as Google.com, Yahoo.com, Bing.com, and YouTube.com can help you find such resources.

BOOKS

Books on Mindfulness

Hanh, T. N. (1992). *Peace is every step: The path of mindfulness in everyday life.* New York, NY: Bantam.

Thich Nhat Hanh (pronounced tic-not-haan) is an internationally known monk, teacher, writer, poet, and peace activist. He is a well-known authority on mindfulness and its application to day-to-day life, and he was nominated for the Nobel Peace Prize by Martin Luther King in 1967. He lives in Plum Village, a monastery that he founded in the South of France after his exile from Vietnam. He has established three monasteries in the United States: in California, New York, and Mississippi. *Peace Is Every Step* is simply written and one of my favorite books by this author. It contains many pearls of wisdom revealed through commentaries and meditations, personal anecdotes, and stories from Nhat Hanh's experiences. It also contains exercises to increase awareness of the body and mind, relationships with others, and the world around us, as well as teachings on establishing peace within oneself and with others and on how to help increase peace in the world. Thich Nhat Hanh is a prolific writer, and many of his books are easy and quick reads. He has written on various subjects. Some of his other books that I have appreciated are *The Miracle of Mindfulness, True Love, Taming the Tiger Within,* and *Mindful Walking.*

Kabat-Zinn, J. (2005). *Full catastrophe living: Using the wisdom of your body and mind to face stress, pain, and illness.* New York, NY: Bantam Dell.

Kabat-Zinn, J. (2005). *Wherever you go, there you are: Mindfulness meditation in everyday life.* New York, NY: Hyperion.

Jon Kabat-Zinn is Professor of Medicine Emeritus and founding director of the Stress Reduction Clinic and the Center for Mindfulness in Medicine, Health Care, and Society at the University of Massachusetts Medical School. His practice of yoga and studies with Buddhist teachers led him to integrate mindfulness with Western science. He is known internationally, and his combination of techniques known as mindfulness-based stress reduction (MBSR) is used in various hospitals, organizations, and retreat centers to help people cope with stress, anxiety, pain, and illness. He continues to teach and lead retreats in the United States and elsewhere. He has an array of audio CDs and books. *Full Catastrophe Living* is a comprehensive book that describes MBSR in detail as it was implemented at the University of Massachusetts Medical Center. It explains mindfulness—its foundation, research, and more—in readable and eloquent language. Anyone with a library of mindfulness materials should consider obtaining a copy. Dr. Kabat-Zinn is a prolific author. Another classic of his to consider is *Wherever You Go, There You Are: Mindfulness Meditation in Everyday Life.* These are well-written excerpts and topics that capture mindfulness, its practice, and its integration into day-to-day life.

Ryan, T. (2012). *A mindful nation.* Carlsbad, CA: Hay House.

Tim Ryan is a congressman from Ohio who has been serving since 2002. In *A Mindful Nation,* he has a clear message: Mindfulness works. He describes his own experiences of stress and discovery of mindfulness and why and how he believes that this simple but effective approach to health and well-being can improve and help children, patients, and soldiers, among others. He is a passionate advocate for the integration of mindfulness approaches in education, health care, and the military. He provides examples of his experiences with mindfulness in his own life and the lives of others.

Segalove, I. (2004). *40 days and 40 nights: Taking time out for self-discovery, a guided journal.* Kansas City, MO: Andrews McMeel.

Irene Segalove is an author who lives in California. *40 Days and 40 Nights* provides a well-structured way to get into the habit of journaling with a mindful and spiritual flavor. Doing something for 40 days can make or break a habit, which can greatly support practice building. It begins with identifying and clarifying your intention, no matter what that intention is, which helps you go about your normal life with more awareness and commitment. Each day includes activities and stories, as well as thoughtful journaling prompts focused on specific topics. Many of the prompts and exercises can increase mindfulness. There are plenty of blank journaling pages for you to record your side of the experiences. You can consider building a practice of mindfulness as your intention and use the book as your mindfulness journal. I recommend that you be selective and choose those practices and prompts that resonate with you the most.

Tolle, E. (1999). *The power of now: A guide to spiritual enlightenment.* Novato, CA: New World Library.

Eckhart Tolle is a German-born Canadian resident, best known as the author of *The Power of Now* and *A New Earth,* which were written in English. He is considered to be an extremely influential spiritual leader both internationally and in the United States. He is not identified with any particular religion, but he has been influenced by a wide range of spiritual works. *The Power of Now* is about personal growth and spirituality. Short and independent yet related excerpts acquaint the reader with various dimensions of spiritual growth. The focus of the book on the "now" enriches the reader's understanding of mindfulness and its practice.

Book on Compassion

Brach, T. (2003). *Radical acceptance: Embracing your life with the heart of a Buddha.* New York, NY: Bantam.

Tara Brach is an American psychologist and expert on Buddhist meditation. She is also the founder and senior teacher of the Insight Meditation Community of Washington, a spiritual community that teaches and practices Vipassana meditation. She teaches Buddhist meditation at many meditation and yoga centers in the United States and Canada. In *Radical Acceptance: Embracing Your Life With the Heart of a Buddha,* she has applied Buddhist teachings such as mindfulness to the psychological process of accepting and healing trauma in simple yet personable and effective language.

Book on Gratitude

Emmons, R. (2007). *Thanks! How practicing gratitude can make you happier.* Boston, MA: Houghton-Mifflin.

Robert Emmons is a professor at the University of California, Davis, and editor-in-chief of the *Journal of Positive Psychology.* His research encompasses personality psychology, the psychology of emotion, and the psychology of religion. His primary interests are in the psychology of gratitude and the psychology of personal goals and how each is related to positive psychological processes including happiness, well-being, and personality integration. He has written several books. *Thanks! How Practicing Gratitude Can Make You Happier* is a readable and engaging book that summarizes the results of his research on gratitude and provides information on incorporating gratitude into day-to-day life.

Book on the Relaxation Response

Benson, H. (2000). *The relaxation response.* New York, NY: Harper Torch.

Herbert Benson is an American cardiologist and founder of the Mind/Body Medical Institute at Massachusetts General Hospital in Boston. Benson is a pioneer in mind/body medicine and one of the first Western physicians to bring spirituality and healing into medicine. He has defined the relaxation response and continues to lead teaching and research into its efficacy in counteracting the harmful effects of stress. His book *The Relaxation Response* (1975, 2000) is well and simply written. It helps the reader understand the science of stress and relaxation, demystifies meditation, and provides guidelines for the practice of meditation as a relaxation response. It truly is a classic as well as a wonderful book for beginners.

Book on Buddhist Philosophy

Kornfield, J. (2008). *The wise heart: A guide to the universal teachings of Buddhist psychology.* New York, NY: Bantam.

Jack Kornfield is a psychologist and a teacher in the Vipassana movement of American Theravada Buddhism. He trained as a Buddhist monk in Thailand, Burma, and India. He is considered one of the leading Buddhist teachers in America and one of the key teachers to introduce mindfulness and Vipassana meditation to the West. His approach emphasizes compassion, loving-kindness, and forgiveness. He is a prolific writer, lecturer, and retreat leader. Descriptions of his books, CDs, classes, and retreats can be found on his website (http://www.jackkornfield.com) and elsewhere. In *The Wise Heart* he describes and draws parallels and differences between Buddhism or Buddhist psychology and Western psychology and illustrates them with wonderful stories, examples, and guidelines. The book makes difficult topics simple, understandable, and accessible.

Books on Yoga

Rama, S., Ballentine, R., & Haynes, A. (2007). *Science of breath: A practical guide*. Honesdale, PA: Himalayan Institute Press.

Swami Rama was an Indian yogi and is well known in the West. He was raised and taught in the Himalayas by a yogi master and was encouraged by him to go to the West. He is especially notable as one of the first yogis to allow himself to be studied by Western scientists. He was examined by scientists at the Menninger Clinic who studied his ability to voluntarily control bodily processes (e.g., heartbeat, blood pressure, body temperature) that are normally considered to be nonvoluntary. He established several ashrams, teaching centers, and charities. A student of both Himalayan cave monasteries and European universities, he founded the Himalayan Institute of Yoga Science and Philosophy to create a bridge between the ancient teachings of the East and modern scientific approaches of the West. He has published several books. *Science of Breath* is an excellent beginning book on breathing techniques and the importance of breath in the practice of yoga. It covers the importance of breathing, basic respiratory physiology, and the relationship between science and yoga.

The Sivananda Yoga Center. (2000). *The Sivananda companion to yoga.* New York, NY: Fireside by Simon & Schuster.

Sivananda Yoga Center (http://www.sivananda.org) is a highly regarded organization for yoga studies and practices that are based on the teachings of Swami Sivananda, one of the greatest yogis of India. His disciple Swami Vishnu Devananda established yoga centers in the West on the basis of Sivananda's teachings. The Sivananda Yoga Center created the first edition of *The Sivananda Companion to Yoga* in 1983. Since its publication, it has sold more than 700,000 copies worldwide and has become a standard text for both yoga students and teachers. The new edition of *The Sivananda Companion to Yoga* remains the classic guide to yoga. With easy-to-follow instructions, inspirational teaching, and detailed illustrations, it covers various aspects of the yoga lifestyle, including relaxation, exercise, dietary guidelines, breathing, and meditation.

Ramacharaka, Yogi. (1930). *Hatha yoga: The yogi philosophy of physical well-being.* Chicago, IL: Yogi Publication Society.
Ramacharaka, Yogi. (1905). *Science of breath.* Chicago, IL: Yogi Publication Society.

There is a fascinating controversy about the writer(s) of these books (see http://users.telenet.be/ananda/ramach.htm). They are attributed to William Walker Atkinson. (http://en.wikipedia.org/wiki/William_Walker_Atkinson). Atkinson was an attorney, merchant, publisher, and author, as well as an occultist and an American pioneer of the New Thought movement. He wrote many books and articles. *Hatha Yoga* and *Science of Breath* are both well and knowledgably written, surprisingly easy to understand, and well received in yoga circles and even in India. *Hatha Yoga* describes what is needed to live a healthy life, physically, psychologically, and spiritually, with simple and detailed instructions of yoga. *Science of Breath* delineates the importance of breath in various aspects of health and provides details of various breathing techniques. Published by the Yogi Publication Society, it is unclear whether an ancient yogi named Ramacharaka ever lived. There are several other notable books on the subject of yoga by the same pseudonym.

Books on General Wisdom

Walsh, R. (1999). *Essential spirituality: The 7 central practices to awaken heart and mind.* New York, NY: Wiley.

Roger Walsh, MD, PhD, is a professor of psychiatry, philosophy, and anthropology, as well as a professor in the religious studies program at the University of California at Irvine. His research and writings span several areas, including the nature of psychological health and well-being, meditation and contemplative practices, religion and spirituality, and wisdom practices. *Essential Spirituality* provides an effective account of seven common principles and practices that are shared among major world religions. Through examples, descriptions, and stories, he provides excellent guidelines for integrating these principles and practices into our daily lives. Over the years, I have read and reread this book and have always found new ways of enriching my practice as a practitioner and as a teacher.

Keyes, K. J. (1987). *Your life is a gift.* Coos Bay, OR: Love Line Books.

Ken Keyes, Jr. was a personal growth author and lecturer and the creator of the Living Love method, a self-help system. He struggled with severe health issues throughout his life and lived a colorful life with multiple personal and professional transitions. He wrote 15 books on personal growth and social consciousness issues, which sold over 4 million copies. He was influenced by Eastern traditions, and his workshops were attended by large numbers of people during the 1970s and 1980s. *Your Life Is a Gift* is a quick read and effective book with short messages illustrated with cartoons. Without using the term *mindfulness,* he conveys the importance of consciousness and especially the way in which "our own expectations" become an impediment to our happiness.

London, E., & Recio, B. (2004). *Sacred rituals: Connecting with spirit through labyrinths, sand paintings, and other traditional arts.* Gloucester, MA: Fair Winds Press.

This is a book about the value and function of rituals and their integration into our lives. It is a well-written and beautifully illustrated book. It is fun, engaging, and informative, especially if you are interested in creating an altar for your practice.

Books With Inspirational Poetry

Hafiz. (1999). *The gift* (D. Ladinsky, Trans.). New York, NY: Penguin Compass.

Hafiz. (1996). *I heard God laughing* (D. Ladinsky, Trans.). Oakland, CA: Mobius Press.

Hafiz. (1996). *The subject tonight is love* (D. Ladinsky, Trans.). New York, NY: Penguin Compass.

Hafiz (pronounced Hafez in Farsi) is a well-known, loved, and cherished mystic poet from 14th-century Persia. Hafiz, a Sufi Master, was acclaimed throughout the Islamic world during his lifetime as well as today. In the West, his work has been recognized by writers such as Thoreau, Goethe, and Ralph Waldo Emerson, who referred to him as "a poet's poet." Daniel Ladinsky's translation has made Hafiz's poetry more popular and accessible in the United States. Hafiz's overarching message through his poetry is love. His poems are beautiful and at times humorous and whimsical. Some Hafiz lovers consider Ladinsky's renditions to be inspired by Hafiz and not real translations. It is difficult to pick a few poems as the best. There are so many wonderful poems that touch the heart, depending on the circumstances. Some of my favorites are "Your Mother and My Mother," "The Subject Tonight Is Love," "It Felt Love," "Ten Thousand Idiots," "Zero," "Someone Who Can Kiss God," and "Someone Should Start Laughing."

O'Donohue, J. (2008). *To bless the space between us: A book of blessings.* New York, NY: Doubleday.

John O'Donohue was an Irish poet, author, priest, and philosopher. He has been widely praised for use of Celtic spiritual traditions to create words of inspiration and wisdom. *To Bless the Space Between Us* includes a blend of poetic language and spiritual insights. O'Donohue looked at life's critical times, such as getting married, having children, starting a new job, losses, or beginnings, and offered guidelines for making the transitions with gorgeous poems.

Rumi. (2004). *The essential Rumi* (C. Barks, Trans.). San Francisco, CA: HarperSanFrancisco.

Jalal ad-Din Muhammad Balkhi, also known as Mowlana and Rumi, was a 13th-century Persian Muslim poet, jurist, theologian, and Sufi mystic. His poetry and spiritual legacy have been greatly appreciated by the East and the West and have transcended national and ethnic borders. His poems have been translated into many of the world's languages and transposed into various formats. Rumi's poetry has gained increasing popularity in America in recent years. He is quoted by many teachers of yoga, Buddhism, mindfulness, and spirituality. One popular translator of his poetry is the poet Coleman Barks, who has published other books on Rumi and was featured on Bill Moyers's PBS television series on poetry. The poetry of Rumi is vast, rich, and at times difficult to grasp. *The Essential Rumi* is a good collection of well-known Rumi poetry. Some of my favorites poems are "A Community of Spirit," "Birdwings," "Elephant in the Dark," "The Guest House," "The Seed Market," and "Out Beyond Ideas of Wrongdoing and Rightdoing," to name a few.

Book of Inspirational Fiction

Gibran, K. (1988). *The prophet*. New Delhi, India: Jaico.

Kahlil (also spelled Khalil) Gibran was a Lebanese–American artist, poet, and writer. He is well known in Arab cultures. He is chiefly known in the English-speaking world for his 1923 masterpiece, *The Prophet,* an early example of inspirational fiction, is about a prophet who discusses life and the human condition. The book is divided into a series of philosophical essays dealing with topics such as love, marriage, children, work, and joy and sorrow. Gibran is the third best-selling poet of all time, behind Shakespeare and Lao-Tzu, the Chinese founder of Taoism. *The Prophet* is illustrated by the author's memorable paintings.

AUDIO CDS

Kabat-Zinn, J. (n.d.). *Audio Series 2* [Audio CD]. http://www.Mindfulness cds.com

See the biographical note on Jon Kabat-Zinn on pp. 254–255. This set of CDs, known as Series 2 (http://www.mindfulnesscds.com/series2 .html), offer meditations and body scans with varying lengths. Several other CDs are also available on the website (mindfulnesscds.com).

Kornfield, J. (2002). *The beginner's guide to forgiveness: How to free your heart and awaken compassion* [Audio CD]. Louisville, CO: Sounds True.

Kornfield, J. (2007). *Guided meditation: Six essential practices to cultivate love, awareness, and wisdom* [Audio CD]. Louisville, CO: Sounds True.

See the biographical note on Jack Kornfield on pp. 258–259. Dr. Kornfield's books, CD's, classes, and retreats can be found on his website (http://www.jackkornfield.com) and elsewhere. Dr. Kornfield has a number of audio CDs with guided meditations. I have enjoyed many of them and have included two examples that I have used.

Goldstein, J. (2007). *Abiding in mindfulness, Volumes 1 and 2* [Audio CD]. Louisville, CO: Sounds True.

Joseph Goldstein has been a well-known and well-respected teacher of Buddhism, mindfulness, insight, and loving-kindness meditations since the 1970s. He is the cofounder of the Insight Meditation Society in Barre, Massachusetts. In *Abiding in Mindfulness, Volumes 1 and 2,* he explains the Satiptthana Sutta, which is the original account of the four foundations of mindfulness as set forward by the Buddha. Anyone who would like to have a more in-depth understanding of the foundations of mindfulness will find these CDs informative, comprehensive, and well done.

Brach, T. (2012). *Mindfulness meditation: Nine guided practices to awaken presence and open your heart* [Audio CD]. Louisville, CO: Sounds True.

See the biographical note on Tara Brach on p. 257. More information on this audio CD can be found online at http://www.soundstrue.com/shop/Mindfulness-Meditation/3954.pd.

DVD

Hanh, T. N. (2008). *Mindful movements* [DVD]. Louisville, CO: Sounds True.

See the biographical note on Thich Nhat Hanh on pp. 253–254. The DVD *Mindful Movements* shows demonstrations of 10 movement exercises that are practiced on a daily basis in Plum Village by Thich Nhat Hanh and the monks who live there. These movements are a great set for daily practice and include gentle stretching and balancing exercises that most people can easily follow. I teach these movements in my classes.

MAGAZINES

Tricycle (http://www.tricycle.com): *Tricycle* is an independent, non-sectarian Buddhist quarterly magazine based in New York City. Most issues have interviews with Buddhist teachers, articles or essays on Buddhism and contemporary issues, book reviews, and a directory of Buddhist centers in the United States.

Yoga Journal (http://www.yogajournal.com): *Yoga Journal* is an American magazine devoted to yoga, food and nutrition, fitness, wellness, and related products. The publisher's website also offers DVDs and related products, as well as a free "yoga sequence builder" for various parts of the body with different levels of difficulty (beginner, intermediate, and advanced levels). The publisher also offers some free videos on YouTube (http://www.youtube.com/user/YogaJournal).

Yoga International (http://www.himalayaninstitute.org): *Yoga International* is a magazine published by the Himalayan Institute. It focuses on teachings of yoga, including physical postures, meditation, holistic health, and environmental issues. The publisher's website also offers a range of other products including DVDs, books, and supplements.

WEBSITES

Center for Compassion and Altruism Research and Education (http://ccare.stanford.edu/): This website provides information, research findings, training, and resources on compassion and compassion-related practices. It is based at Stanford University in California.

Center for Mindfulness in Medicine, Healthcare, and Society (http://www.umassmed.edu/cfm/home/index.aspx): This comprehensive website provides information on teaching, training, research, and workshops on mindfulness, among other offerings. Under the section "Other MBSR Programs Worldwide," you can find local information on mindfulness practitioners close to your home.

Dharma Seed (http://www.dharmaseed.org): Dharma Seed is a nonprofit organization dedicated to preserving and sharing the spoken teachings of Theravada Buddhism in modern languages. The website provides free access to talks and recordings by well-known teachers, with an option for donations.

Himalayan Institute (http://www.himalayaninstitute.org): The Himalayan Institute is an international nonprofit organization that promotes yoga and holistic health through yoga retreats, residential programs, health products and services, media publications, and humanitarian projects. The institute's main campus is located in the Pocono Mountains of northeastern Pennsylvania and is the site for most of its residential programming. Branch centers also operate in Cameroon, India, Great Britain, Malaysia, and Mexico. The organization was founded by Swami Rama of the Himalayas. The organization's current website provides free education on meditation posture (http://www.himalayaninstitute.org/study-online/free-content/learning-meditation/).

Insight Meditation Community of Washington DC (http://www.imcw.org): The Insight Meditation Community of Washington (IMCW) is a spiritual community that teaches and practices Insight/Vipassana meditation in the Washington, DC, metro area. It offers a number of retreats and programs. The main teacher is Tara Brach, who is well known and respected in the community and nationally. The site also offers free access to talks and other related information on meditation practices.

Insight Meditation Society (http://www.dharma.org): The Insight Meditation Society (IMS) is a nonprofit organization for the study of Buddhism located in Barre, Massachusetts. It was founded by Jack Kornfield, Sharon Salzberg, and Joseph Goldstein and is rooted in the Theravada tradition. IMS meditation practices are based on the teachings of the late Burmese monk Mahasi Sayadaw. The center offers several meditation courses in varying length. Some are designed only for the experienced practitioner.

Kripalu Center for Yoga and Health (http://www.kripalu.org): Kripalu is a nonprofit organization located in Stockbridge, Massachusetts. The programs emphasize yoga, nutrition, and the Eastern tradition of Ayurveda for health and well-being. The center offers workshops, trainings, and classes.

Laboratory for Affective Neuroscience (http://psyphz.psych. wisc.edu/web/index.html): The Laboratory for Affective Neuroscience engages in a broad program of research on the brain mechanisms underlying emotion and emotion regulation, including the mechanisms of mind–brain–body interaction.

National Center for Complementary and Alternative Medicine (http://www.nccam.nih.gov): This website provides information on a group of diverse medical and health care systems, practices, and products that are not generally considered part of conventional medicine on topics from A to Z ("acupuncture to zinc"). For example, under "M" you will find meditation. Information about mindfulness is currently provided under meditation. For each entry, there is a definition and supporting research as well as other relevant information.

Omega Institute for Holistic Studies (http://www.eomega. org): Omega is a nonprofit retreat center located in Rhinebeck, New York. Omega's workshops, conferences, and retreats aim to create dialogues on the integration of modern medicine and natural healing; connect science, spirituality, and creativity; and build the groundwork for new traditions and lifestyles. Omega also provides programs in New York City and during the winter in Costa Rica. Various workshops and retreats are provided with well-known teachers.

Plum Village (http://www.plumvillage.org) and **Blue Cliff Monastery** (http://www.bluecliffmonastery.org): Plum village is a Buddhist meditation center and the home of Thich Nhat Hanh in the South of France. Blue Cliff Monastery in New York is an extension of Plum Village. It offers information, retreats, talks, and programs.

Self-Realization Fellowship (SRF; http://www.yogananda-srf. org): The SRF is a worldwide organization founded by the well-known yogi and guru, Paramahasana Yogananda, in Los Angeles, California. Yogananda was very influential in bringing the teachings of yoga to the West. He was a prolific writer, and his book, *The Autobiography of a Yogi,* received a lot of attention. The goal of the organization is to make the teachings of Kriya yoga available to the public. The teachings of Paramahasana, which include meditation techniques, Kriya yoga, and various aspects of a balanced spiritual living, are available through the SRF in the form of lessons as a home-study series for a very modest cost. The SRF offers information and programs in a number of locations and countries.

Spirit Rock Meditation Center (http://www.spiritrock.org): The center is located in Woodacre, California and is dedicated to Buddhist teachings in the Vipassana tradition, the practice of mindful awareness called insight meditation. The center provides silent meditation retreats, classes, and trainings for both new and experienced students.

Sounds True (http://www.soundstrue.com/shop/welcome): Sounds True is a multimedia publishing company based in Louisville, Colorado. The company has published audio recordings, books, music, filmed events, multimedia packages, and online educational programs from people prominent in the fields of spirituality, meditation, psychology, and holistic health. The company offers free interviews on its website. A sample of its offerings can also be viewed on YouTube (http://www.youtube.com/user/SoundsTrueVideos).

3HO Foundation: Healthy, Happy, Holy Organization (http://www.3ho.org): This website presents information about Kundalini yoga practices and teachings as taught by Yogi Bhajan, a spiritual leader and a highly successful entrepreneur. Kundalini yoga is more active than the more common Hatha yoga, with a focus on extensive breathing exercises, pose, and mantra repetitions. Spirit Voyage (http://www.spiritvoyage.com) is an online store that offers books, tapes, music, DVDs, and clothing related to Kundalini yoga practices.

REFERENCES

Andersen, A. (2007). Stories I tell my patients: Where are you when you are eating? *Eating Disorders: The Journal of Treatment & Prevention, 15*, 279–280. doi:10.1080/10640260701323557

Arrien, A. (2007). *The second half of life: Opening the eight gates of wisdom.* Louisville, CO: Sounds True.

Baer, R. (2003). Mindfulness training as a clinical intervention: A conceptual and empirical review. *Clinical Psychology: Science and Practice, 10*, 125–143. doi:10.1093/clipsy.bpg015

Ballentine, R. (1999). *Transition to vegetarianism: An evolutionary step.* Honesdale, PA: Himalayan Institute Press.

Becker, I. (2000). *Uses of yoga in psychiatry and medicine.* Washington, DC: American Psychiatric Press.

Benson, H. (2000). *The relaxation response.* New York, NY: Harper Torch.

Benson, H., Beary, J. F., & Carol, M. P. (1974). The relaxation response. *Psychiatry, 37*, 37–46.

Bernardi, L., Porta, C., & Sleight, P. (2006). Cardiovascular, cerebrovascular, and respiratory changes induced by different types of music in musicians and nonmusicians: The importance of silence. *Heart, 92,* 445–452. doi:10.1136/hrt.2005.064600

Bernstein, D., Borkovec, T., & Hazlett-Stevens, H. (2000). *New directions in progressive relaxation training: A guidebook for helping professionals.* Westport, CT: Praeger.

Block, R. A., Arnott, D. P., Quigley, B., & Lynch, W. C. (1989). Unilateral nostril breathing influences lateralized cognitive performance. *Brain and Cognition, 9,* 181–190. doi:10.1016/0278-2626(89)90028-6

Boccio, F. J. (2004). *Mindfulness yoga: The awakened union of breath, body, and mind.* Boston, MA: Wisdom.

Bodhananda, M. S. (1995). *Swara yoga.* Bihar, India: Bihar School of Yoga.

Bono, G., McCullough, M. E., & Root, L. M. (2008). Forgiveness, feeling connected to others, and well-being: Two longitudinal studies. *Personality and Social Psychology Bulletin, 34,* 182–195. doi:10.1177/0146167207310025

Brach, T. (2003). *Radical acceptance: Embracing your life with the heart of a Buddha.* New York, NY: Bantam.

Brown, R. P., & Gerberg, P. L. (2005a). Sudarshan Kriya yogic breathing in the treatment of stress, anxiety, and depression, Part I: Neurophysiologic model. *Journal of Alternative and Complementary Medicine, 11,* 189–201. doi:10.1089/acm.2005.11.189

Brown, R. P., & Gerberg, P. L. (2005b). Sudarshan Kriya yogic breathing in the treatment of stress, anxiety, and depression, Part II: Clinical application and guidelines. *Journal of Alternative and Complementary Medicine, 11,* 711–717. doi:10.1089/acm.2005.11.711

Bushell, W. C. (2009). Longevity: Potential lifespan and health span enhancement through practice of the basic yoga meditation regimen. *Annals of the New York Academy of Sciences, 1172,* 20–27. doi:10.1111/j.1749-6632.2009.04538.x

Chida, Y., & Steptoe, A. (2009). The association of anger and hostility with future coronary heart disease: A meta-analysis of prospective evidence. *Journal of the American College of Cardiology, 53,* 936–946. doi:10.1016/j.jacc.2008.11.044

Chida, Y., & Steptoe, A. (2010). Greater cardiovascular responses to laboratory mental stress are associated with poor subsequent cardiovascular risk status: A meta analysis of prospective evidence.

Hypertension, 55, 1026–1032. doi:10.1161/HYPERTENSION AHA.109.146621

Chodron, P. (2001). *Start where you are.* Boston, MA: Shambhala.

Coffey, K., Hartman, M., & Fredrickson, B. (2010). Deconstructing mindfulness and constructing mental health: Understanding mindfulness and its mechanisms of action. *Mindfulness, 1,* 235–253. doi:10.1007/s12671-010-0033-2

Cohen, S., Janicki-Deverts, D., & Miller, G. E. (2007). Psychological stress and disease. *JAMA, 298,* 1685–1687. doi:10.1001/jama.298.14.1685

Danner, D. D., Snowdon, D. A., & Friesen, W. V. (2001). Positive emotions in early life and longevity: Findings from a nun study. *Journal of Personality and Social Psychology, 80,* 804–813. doi:10.1037/0022-3514.80.5.804

Davidson, R. J. (2010). Empirical explorations of mindfulness: Conceptual and methodological conundrums. *Emotion, 10,* 8–11. doi:10.1037/a0018480

Davidson, R. J., Kabat-Zinn, J., Schumacher, J., Rosenkranz, M., Muller, D., Santorelli, S. F., ... Sheridan, J. F. (2003). Alterations in brain and immune function produced by mindfulness meditation. *Psychosomatic Medicine, 65,* 564–570. doi:10.1097/01.PSY.0000077505.67574.E3

Davis, D. M., & Hayes, J. (2011). What are the benefits of mindfulness? A practice review of psychotherapy-related research. *Psychotherapy, 48,* 198–208. doi:10.1037/a0022062

Davis, M. C., Zautra, A. J., & Smith, B. W. (2004). Chronic pain, stress, and the dynamics of affective differentiation. *Journal of Personality, 72,* 1133–1160. doi:10.1111/j.1467-6494.2004.00293.x

Devereux, P. G., & Heffner, K. L. (2007). Psychophysiological approaches to the study of laughter: Toward an integration with positive psychology. In A. D. Ong & M. H. M. van Dulmen (Eds.), *Oxford handbook of methods in positive psychology* (pp. 233–249). New York, NY: Oxford University Press.

Dossey, L. (2008). Quiet, please: Observations on noise. *Explore, 4,* 157–163.

Emmons, R. (2007). *Thanks!* Boston, MA: Houghton Mifflin.

Enright, R. (1996). Counseling within the forgiveness triad: On forgiving, receiving forgiveness, and self-forgiveness. *Counseling and Values, 40,* 107–126. doi:10.1002/j.2161-007X.1996.tb00844.x

Enright, R. (2001). *Forgiveness is a choice: A step-by-step process for resolving anger and restoring hope.* Washington, DC: APA LifeTools.

Evans, K., Dougherty, D. D., Schmid, A. M., Scannell, E., McCallister, A., Benson, H., . . . Lazar, S. W. (2009). Modulation of spontaneous breathing via limbic/paralimbic-bulbar circuitry: An event-related fMRI study. *Neuroimage, 47,* 961–971.

Feiss, H. (1999). *Essential monastic wisdom: Writings on contemplative life.* San Francisco, CA: HarperCollins.

Frankl, V. (1959). *Man's search for meaning.* Boston, MA: Beacon Press.

Fredrickson, B. L. (2001). The role of positive emotions in positive psychology. *American Psychologist, 56,* 218–226. doi:10.1037/0003-066X.56.3.218

Fredrickson, B. L. (2004). The broaden-and-build theory of positive emotions. *Philosophical Transactions of the Royal Society of London, 359,* 1367–1377. doi:10.1098/rstb.2004.1512

Fredrickson, B. L., Cohn, M. A., & Finkel, S. M. (2008). Open hearts build lives: Positive emotions, induced through loving-kindness meditation, build consequential personal resources. *Journal of Personality and Social Psychology, 95,* 1045–1062. doi:10.1037/a0013262

Friborg, J. T., Yuan, J.-M., Wang, R., Koh, W.-P., Lee, H.-P., & Yu, M. C. (2008). Incense use and respiratory tract carcinomas: A prospective cohort study. *Cancer, 113,* 1676–1684. doi:10.1002/cncr.23788

Friedberg J. P., Suchday S., & Srinivas, V. S. (2009). Relationship between forgiveness and psychological and physiological indices in cardiac patients. *International Journal of Behavioral Medicine, 16,* 205–211.

Gibran, K. (1988). *The prophet.* New Delhi, India: Jaico.

Goldstein, J. (2003). *Insight meditation: The practice of freedom.* Boston, MA: Shambhala.

Goldstein J. (2007). *Abiding in mindfulness, Volumes 1 and 2* [Audio CD]. Louisville, CO: Sounds True.

Gunaratana, B. (2012). *The four foundations of mindfulness in plain English.* Somerville, MA: Wisdom.

Goetz, J. L., Keltner, D., & Simon-Thomas, E. (2010). Compassion: An evolutionary analysis and empirical review. *Psychological Bulletin, 136,* 351–374. doi:10.1037/a0018807

Gorman, J. (2011, September 14). Laughter is a physical, not a mental thing study suggests. *The New York Times.*

Green, J. (1994). *Integrative meditation: Towards unity of body, mind, & spirit.* Falls Church, VA: James Wyche Green.

Grossman, P., Niemann, L., Schmidt, S., & Walach, H. (2004). Mindfulness-based stress reduction and health benefits: A meta-analysis. *Journal of Psychosomatic Research, 57*, 35–43. doi:10.1016/S0022-3999(03)00573-7

Hanh, T. N. (1992a). *The miracle of mindfulness.* Boston, MA: Beacon Press.

Hanh, T. N. (1992b). *Peace is every step: The path of mindfulness in everyday life.* New York, NY: Bantam.

Hanh, T. N. (2002). *Anger: Wisdom for cooling the flames.* New York, NY: Riverhead Books.

Hanh, T. N. (2008). *Mindful movements* [DVD]. Louisville, CO: Sounds True.

Hanh, T. N., & Cheung, L. (2010). *Savor: Mindful eating, mindful life.* New York, NY: HarperCollins.

Hayes, S. C. (2002). Acceptance, mindfulness, and science. *Clinical Psychology: Science and Practice, 9*, 101–106. doi:10.1093/clipsy.9.1.101

Hayes, S. C., Luoma, J. B., Bond, F. W., Masuda, A., & Lillis, J. (2006). Acceptance and commitment therapy: Model, process and outcomes. *Behaviour Research and Therapy, 44*, 1–25. doi:10.1016/j.brat.2005.06.006

Hayes, S. C., Strosahl, K., & Wilson, K. G. (1999). *Acceptance and commitment therapy.* New York, NY: Guilford Press.

Higashi, M. (1964). Pranayama as a psychiatric regimen. *The Lancet, 284*, 1177–1178. doi:10.1016/S0140-6736(64)92703-5

Hofmann, S. G., Grossman, P., & Hinton, D. (2011). Loving-kindness and compassion meditation: Potential for psychological interventions. *Clinical Psychology Review, 31*, 1126–1132. doi:10.1016/j.cpr.2011.07.003

Hofmann, S. G., Sawyer, A. T., Witt, A. A., & Oh, D. (2010). The effect of mindfulness-based therapy on anxiety and depression: A meta-analytic review. *Journal of Counseling and Clinical Psychology, 78*, 169–183.

Hölzel, B. K., Carmody, J., Evans, K. C., Hoge, E. A., Dusek, J. A., Morgan, L., . . . Lazar, S. W. (2010). Stress reduction correlates with structural changes in the amygdala. *Social Cognitive and Affective Neuroscience, 5*, 11–17.

Hölzel, B. K., Carmody, J., Vangel, M., Congleton, C., Yerramsetti, S. M., Gard, T., & Lazar, S. W. (2011). Mindfulness practice leads to increases in regional brain gray matter density. *Psychiatry Research: Neuroimaging, 191,* 36–43. doi:10.1016/j.pscychresns.2010.08.006

Hölzel, B. K., Ott, U., Gard, T., Hempel, H., Weygandt, M., Morgen, K., & Vaitl, D. (2008). Investigation of mindfulness meditation practitioners with voxel-based morphometry. *Social Cognitive and Affective Neuroscience, 3,* 55–61. doi:10.1093/scan/nsm038

Jacobs, T. L., Epel, E. S., Lin, J., Blackburn, E. H., Wolkowitz, O. M., Bridwell, D. A., . . . Saron, C. D. (2011). Intensive meditation training, immune cell telomerase activity, and psychological mediators. *Psychoneuroendocrinology, 36,* 664–681.

Jacobson, E. (1929). *Progressive relaxation.* Chicago, IL: The University of Chicago Press.

Jina, S. (2003). Silence: A Dharma talk given by sister Jina on September 1, 2002. *The Mindfulness Bell: A Journal of the Art of Mindful Living, 35,* 39–43.

Kabat-Zinn, J. (2003). Mindfulness-based interventions in context: Past, present, future. *Clinical Psychology: Science and Practice, 10,* 144–156. doi:10.1093/clipsy.bpg016

Kabat-Zinn, J. (2005). *Full catastrophe living: Using the wisdom of your body and mind to face stress, pain, and illness.* New York, NY: Bantam Dell.

Kabat-Zinn, J., Wheeler, E., Light, T., Skillings, A., Scharf, M., Cropley, T., . . . Bernhard, J. (1998). Influence of a mindfulness based stress reduction intervention on rates of skin clearing in patients with moderate to severe psoriasis undergoing phototherapy (UVB) and photochemotherapy (PUVA). *Psychosomatic Medicine, 60,* 625–632.

Kasl, C. (1999). *If the Buddha dated.* New York, NY: Penguin Books.

Keyes, K. J. (1975). *Handbook of higher consciousness.* Berkeley, CA: Living Love Center.

Keyes, K. J. (1987). *Your life is a gift.* Coos Bay, OR: Love Line Books.

Keyes, K. J. (1995). *Your road map to lifelong happiness.* Coos Bay, OR: Love Line Books.

Khalsa, S. K. (2001). *Kundalini yoga: Unlock your inner potential through life-changing exercise.* New York, NY: Dorling Kindersley.

Khalsa, S. P. K. (1966). *Kundalini yoga: The flow of eternal power.* New York, NY: Berkley.

Kiecolt-Glaser, J. K. (2009). Psychoneuroimmunology psychology's gateway to the biomedical future. *Perspectives on Psychological Science, 4,* 367–369. doi:10.1111/j.1745-6924.2009.01139.x

Klein, R., Pilon, D., Prosser, S., & Shannahoff-Khalsa, D. (1986). Nasal airflow asymmetries and human performance. *Biological Psychology, 23,* 127–137. doi:10.1016/0301-0511(86)90077-3

Kornfield, J. (2002). *The beginner's guide to forgiveness: How to free your heart and awaken compassion* [Audio CD]. Louisville, CO: Sounds True.

Kornfield, J. (2007). *Guided meditation: Six essential practices to cultivate love, awareness, and wisdom* [Audio CD]. Louisville, CO: Sounds True.

Kornfield, J. (2008). *The wise heart: A guide to the universal teachings of Buddhist psychology.* New York, NY: Bantam.

Kraftsow, G. (1999). *Yoga for wellness.* New York, NY: Penguin.

Kristeller, J. L., Baer, R. A., & Quillian-Wolver, R. (2006). Mindfulness-based approaches to eating disorders. In R. A. Baer (Ed.), *Mindfulness-based treatment approaches: Clinician's guide to evidence base and applications* (pp. 75–91). San Diego, CA: Elsevier Academic Press. doi:10.1016/B978-012088519-0/50005-8

Kubzansky, L. D., Davidson, W., & Rozanski, A. (2005). The clinical impact of negative psychological states: Expanding the spectrum of risk for coronary artery disease. *Psychosomatic Medicine, 67*(Suppl. 1), S10–S14. doi:10.1097/01.psy.0000164012.88829.41

Ladd, V. (2009). *Ayurveda: The science of self-healing: A practical guide.* Twin Lakes, WI: Lotus Press.

Lawler, K. A., Younger, J. W., Piferi, R. L., Jobe, R. L., Edmondson, K. A., & Jones, W. H. (2005). The unique effects of forgiveness on health: an exploration of pathways. *Journal of Behavioral Medicine, 28*(2), 157–167. doi:10.1007/s10865-005-3665-2

Lawler-Row, K. A., Karremans, J. C., Scott, C., Edlis-Matityahou, M., & Edwards, L. (2008). Forgiveness, physiological reactivity and health: The role of anger. *International Journal of Psychophysiology, 68,* 51–58. doi:10.1016/j.ijpsycho.2008.01.001

Lazar, S. W., Kerr, C., Wasserman, R. H., Gray, J. R., Greve, D., Treadway, M. T., . . . Fischl, B. (2005). Meditation experience is associated with increased cortical thickness. *Neuroreport, 16,* 1893–1897. doi:10.1097/01.wnr.0000186598.66243.19

Leonard, G., & Murphy, M. (1995). *The life we are given: A long-term program for realizing the potential of the body, mind, heart, and soul.* New York, NY: Putnam Books.

Linehan, M. M. (1993). *Cognitive-behavior treatment of borderline personality disorder.* New York, NY: Guilford Press.

Lutz, A., Brefczynski-Lewis, J., Johnstone, T., & Davidson, R. J. (2008). Regulation of the neural circuitry of emotion by compassion meditation: Effects of meditative expertise. *PLoS ONE, 3*(3), e1897. doi:10.1371/journal.pone.0001897

Lutz, A., Dunne, J. D., & Davidson, R. J. (2007). Meditation and the neuroscience of consciousness: An introduction. In P. Zelazo, M. Moscovitch, & E. Thompson (Eds.), *Cambridge handbook of consciousness* (pp. 499–551). New York, NY: Cambridge University Press.

Lutz, A., Greischar, L. L., Perlman, D. M., & Davidson, R. J. (2009). BOLD signal in insula is differentially related to cardiac function during compassion meditation in experts vs. novices. *NeuroImage, 47,* 1038–1046. doi:10.1016/j.neuroimage.2009.04.081

Lutz, A., Greischar, L. L., Rawlings, N. B., Ricard, M., & Davidson, R. J. (2004). Long-term meditators self-induce high amplitude-gamma synchrony during mental practice. *Proceedings of the National Academy of Sciences, USA, 101,* 16369–16373. doi:10.1073/pnas.0407401101

Mehta, M. (1994). *How to use yoga: A step-by-step guide to the Iyengar method of yoga for relaxation, health, and well-being.* New York, NY: Smithmark.

Miller, M., & Fry, W. F. (2009). The effect of mirthful laughter on the human cardiovascular system. *Medical Hypotheses, 73,* 636–639.

Mindfulness training and emotion regulation: Clinical and neuroscience perspectives [Special section]. (2010). *Emotion, 10,* 1–92.

Moore, T. (2003). *The soul's religion: Cultivating a profoundly spiritual way of life.* New York, NY: HarperCollins.

Morningstar, A. D., & Urmila, D. (2008). *The ayurvedic cookbook: A personalized guide to good nutrition and health.* Twin Lakes, WI: Lotus Press.

Nauert, R. (2010, November 5). *Meditation associated with improved cell function.* PsychCentral. Available at http://psychcentral.com/news/2010/11/05/meditation-associated-with-improved-cell-function/20566.html

Newberg, A. B., Wintering, N., Waldman, M., Amen, D., Khalsa, D., & Alavi, A. (2010). Cerebral blood flow differences between long-term meditators and nonmeditators. *Consciousness and Cognition, 19,* 899–905. doi:10.1016/j.concog.2010.05.003

Olivo, E. L. (2009). Protection through the lifespan. *Annals of the New York Academy of Sciences, 1172,* 163–171. doi:10.1111/j.1749-6632.2009.04415.x

Owen, A. D., Hayward, R. D., & Toussaint, L. L. (2011, April). *Forgiveness and immune functioning in people living with HIV-AIDS.* Paper presented at the 32nd annual meeting of the Society for Behavioral Medicine, Washington, DC.

Pace, T. W. W., Negi, L. T., Adame, D. D., Cole, S. P., Sivilli, T. I., Brown, T. D., . . . Raison, C. L. (2009). Effect of compassion meditation on neuroendocrine, innate immune and behavioral responses to psychosocial stress. *Psychoneuroendocrinology, 34,* 87–98.

Paul, R. (2004). *The yoga of sound: Tapping the hidden power of music and chant.* Novato, CA: New World Library.

Provine, R. R. (2000). *Laughter: A scientific investigation.* New York, NY: Viking Penguin.

Rama, S., Ballentine, R., & Haynes, A. (2007). *Science of breath: A practical guide.* Honesdale, PA: The Himalayan Institute Press.

Ramacharaka, Y. (1905). *Science of breath.* Chicago, IL: Yogi Publication Society.

Ramacharaka, Y. (1931). *Fourteen lessons in yogi philosophy.* Chicago, IL: Yoga Publication Society.

Raman, K. (1998). *A matter of health: Integration of yoga and western medicine for prevention and cure.* Chennai, India: EastWest Books.

Rinpoche, S. (2002). *The Tibetan book of living and dying.* New York, NY: HarperCollins.

Rosenthal, N. (2011). *Transcendence: Healing and transformation through transcendental meditation.* New York, NY: Penguin Books.

Ryan, T. (2012). *A mindful nation.* Carlsbad, CA: Hay House.

Salzberg, S. (1995). *Loving-kindness.* Boston, MA: Shambhala.

Sapolsky, R. M. (1998). *Why zebras don't get ulcers: An updated guide to stress, stress-related diseases, and coping.* New York, NY: W. H. Freeman.

Saraswati, N. S. (2002). *Prana, pranayama, prana vidya.* Bihar, India: Yoga Publications Trust.

Schiffmann, E. (1996). *Yoga: The spirit and practice of moving into stillness.* New York, NY: Simon & Schuster.

Schwartz, M. S., & Olson, R. P. (2003). A historical perspective on the field of biofeedback and applied psychophysiology. In M. S. Schwartz & F. Andrasik (Eds.), *Biofeedback: A practitioner's guide* (3rd ed., pp. 3–19). New York, NY: Guilford Press.

Segal, Z., William, M., & Teasdale, J. (2001). *Mindfulness-based cognitive therapy for depression: A new approach to preventing relapse.* New York, NY: Guilford Press.

Segerstrom, S. C., & Miller, G. E. (2004). Psychological stress and the human immune system: A meta-analytic study of 30 years of inquiry. *Psychological Bulletin, 130,* 601–630. doi:10.1037/0033-2909.130.4.601

Seybold, K. S., Hill, P. C., Neumann, J. K., & Chi, D. S. (2001). Physiological and psychological correlates of forgiveness. *Journal of Psychology and Christianity, 20,* 250–259.

Shannahoff-Khalsa, D. S. (2007). Selective unilateral autonomic activation: Implications for psychiatry. *CNS Spectrums, 12,* 625–634.

Shannahoff-Khalsa, D. S., Boyle, M. R., & Buebel, M. E. (1991). The effects of unilateral forced nostril breathing on cognition. *International Journal of Neuroscience, 57,* 239–249. doi:10.3109/00207459109150697

Siegel, D. (2007). *The mindful brain: Reflection and attunement in the cultivation of well-being.* New York, NY: Norton.

Sivananda Yoga Center. (2000). *The Sivananda companion to yoga.* New York, NY: Simon & Schuster.

Steptoe, A., Dockray, S., & Wardle, J. (2009). Positive affect and psychobiological processes relevant to health. *Journal of Personality, 77,* 1747–1776. doi:10.1111/j.1467-6494.2009.00599.x

Strean, W. B. (2009). Laughter prescription. *Canadian Family Physician, 55,* 965–967.

Surya Das, L. (2007). *Buddha is as Buddha does: The ten original practices for enlightened living.* San Francisco, CA: HarperSanFrancisco.

Telles, S., Raghuraj, P., Maharana, S., & Nagendra, H. R. (2007). Immediate effect of three yoga breathing techniques on performance on a letter-cancellation task. *Perceptual and Motor Skills, 104,* 1289–1296. doi:10.2466/pms.104.4.1289-1296

Toussaint, L. L., Owen, A. D., & Cheadle, A. (2012). Forgive to live: Forgiveness, health, and longevity. *Journal of Behavioral Medicine, 35,* 375–386.

Tugade, M. M., Fredrickson, B. L., & Feldman Barrett, L. (2004). Psychological resilience and positive emotional granularity: Examining the benefits of positive emotions on coping and health. *Journal of Personality, 72,* 1161–1190.

Urry, H. L., van Reekum, C. M., Johnstone, T., Thurow, M. E., Burghy, C. A., Mueller, C. J., & Davidson, R. J. (2003). *Neural correlates of voluntarily regulating negative affect* (Report No. 725.18). San Diego, CA: Society for Neuroscience.

Vaillant, G. E. (2008). Positive emotions, spirituality and the practice of psychiatry. *Mens Sana Monographs, 6,* 48–62.

Vishnu-Devananda, S. (1988). *The complete illustrated book of yoga.* New York, NY: Three Rivers Press.

Voisin, J., Bidet-Caulet, A., Bertrand, O., & Fonlupt, P. (2006). Listening in silence activates auditory areas: A functional magnetic resonance imaging study. *The Journal of Neuroscience, 26,* 273–278. doi:10.1523/JNEUROSCI.2967-05.2006

Walsh, R. (1999). *Essential spirituality: The 7 central practices to awaken heart and mind.* New York, NY: Wiley.

Weil, A. (2000). *Breathing: The master key to self-healing* [Audio CD]. Louisville, CO: Sounds True.

Wilber, K. (2007). *The integral vision.* Boston, MA: Shambhala.

Willich, S. N., Wegscheider, K., Stallmann, M., & Keil, T. (2006). Noise burden and the risk of myocardial infarction. *European Heart Journal, 27,* 276–282. doi:10.1093/eurheartj/ehi658

Wolf, B. (2005, May 13). *Laughter may be the best medicine.* New York, NY: ABC News.

Xu, J., & Roberts, R. (2010). The power of positive emotions: It's a matter of life or death—subjective well being and longevity over 28 years in a general population. *Health Psychology, 29,* 9–19. doi:10.1037/a0016767

Zautra, A. J., Affleck, G. G., Tennen, H., Reich, J. W., & Davis, M. C. (2005). Dynamic approaches to emotions and stress in everyday life: Bolger and Zuckerman reloaded with positive as well as negative affects. *Journal of Personality, 73,* 1512–1538.

Zautra, A. J., Davis, M. C., & Smith, B. W. (2004). Emotions, personality, and health: Introduction to the special issue. *Journal of Personality, 72,* 1097–1104. doi:10.1111/j.1467-6494.2004.00291.x

INDEX

ABOUT THE AUTHOR

Rezvan Ameli, PhD, is a senior clinical psychologist who has extensive research, clinical, and teaching experience. For the past 12 years, she has worked at the National Institute of Mental Health (NIMH), where she provides clinical training for diagnosing and measuring mood and anxiety disorders. In addition to being licensed as a psychologist, she is certified as a cognitive therapist by the Academy of Cognitive Therapy and has received training from the Beck Institute for Cognitive Therapy.

Prior to working at the NIMH, Dr. Ameli provided clinical and administrative services, as well as teaching and conducting research, at Yale–New Haven Hospital and Hartford Hospital. She has held academic positions at Yale University, the University of Connecticut, and Howard University. She has worked with diverse clinical populations and age groups and has developed several clinical programs. She has also collaborated on more than 20 research projects and published about 30 journal articles.

Dr. Ameli has been studying mindfulness, yoga, and yoga philosophy for over a decade. She volunteers her services to the National Institutes of Health community and the public in applying mindfulness and meditative practices to reduce stress and enhance the quality of life. For her commitment to promoting employee productivity and well-being by reducing stress at the workplace, she received the NIMH Director's Award.